The Modern Preserver's Kitchen

Cooking with Jam, Chutney,
Pickles and Ferments

Susan

hope you enjoy

Kylee Newton

Photography by
Laura Edwards

Kylee Newton

Hardie Grant

QUADRILLE

Contents

... from one thing comes another ...

For the past ten years, exploring the many avenues of preserving has been my passion. I started by making chutney, which evolved into jams, pickles, ferments and drinks. In this book, I hope to take you on a similar journey, to share with you what I have learnt along the way and to inspire you to use what you make in your everyday cooking.

Nine years ago, I started a small, handmade preserving business in East London called Newton & Pott. Not only did I want to make delicious, small-batch preserves using excellent produce, but I also sought to show people the place that preserving has in our history, and to represent it within a modern context.

People have preserved food for thousands of years. You can see it in countless countries and cultures across the globe. It's been a means of feeding people in unfruitful times, and also sometimes relied upon for survival. Like all food, it brings people together: from the passing down of these culinary traditions comes community and identity.

For me, preserving is sustainable cooking at its best. It makes the most of each season's offering, giving yield longevity and creating a type of edible time capsule. All of this is good for the planet, which is one of the main reasons I'm so attracted to the process. Reducing waste and making the most of the seasons are at the heart of my moral compass, as pagan as that sounds...

I grew up in New Zealand in the late '70s and '80s. From a young age, the idea of being a "Tidy Kiwi" was drummed into me, thanks to a government campaign to reduce litter. Watching *Sesame Street*, I learned about recycling by following the journey of a newspaper, from the delivery boy tossing a rolled-up issue of the day's news onto a doorstep, which was duly read and discarded, before making its way to the paper factory where it was transformed into a new issue of the next day's news. Fascinated, I begged for a paper-recycling kit that Christmas. These beginnings gave me an appreciation and respect for the planet that I still hold close.

I also grew up eating what was in season. I knew that if we couldn't get tomatoes, it wasn't summer. Coming from a small town on a small island at the bottom of the world, we didn't have access to mass imported produce from abroad. We ate what was grown and reared around us. My father was a fisherman, so his catch of the day was often on the table that evening.

Over the decades, we have become disconnected from the planet – we have become accustomed to buying produce out of season; to ingredients grown for quantity, not quality; and to perfectly formed, unblemished fruit and vegetables, thanks to human interventions and industrial farming. The Earth is in an environmental crisis. This behaviour has depleted its ability to repair itself, and young people today seem to be better informed and aware of the dangers facing our world than past generations have been. They don't want to inherit a planet in tatters, but rather a healthy environment to pass on to their own children. We must all be accountable in our own lives and take responsibility for our lifestyle choices. This starts by switching to locally grown produce, taking an interest in where our food comes from and making better choices about how we buy it; it comes from making more things from scratch, creating less waste and using fewer resources.

Just a disclaimer here: I am far from perfect. I'm neither vegan nor vegetarian. I have thrown food out if it's going bad, and I sometimes find myself with single-use plastic in the house! I find myself in the supermarket when I don't want to make my own pasta or bread, if I want cheap alcohol, or cow's milk or cream to bake with. But my husband and I make conscious, achievable steps to try to lower our carbon footprint.

Obviously, we preserve: the spring's radishes become pickles, summertime peaches are made into jam to enable them to be eaten at any time of year. We make a stock list of what we have in the house and only buy essentials to top it up – there's very little waste. We take reusable bags when we go shopping and refuse plastic bags when offered them. We buy from our local butcher and fishmonger, supporting local markets and producers. We compost our food scraps and wash out single-use plastic to use again. I even wash and dry my baking paper to make it last another day.

My intention with this book is to help you start this dialogue, with yourself and others, so you too can contribute to food sustainability, starting with what you eat every day – by preserving what's in season and using these preserves or what's in your fridge as a base for making easy family meals.

How to use this book

"How do I eat it?" A question I've heard countless times from customers of my market stall over the years. With this in mind, I've been working on ideas that incorporate preserves into menus and meals for some time. In my first book, *The Modern Preserver*, I made suggestions for enjoying your newly made preserves beyond the parameters they are traditionally assigned – on toast or in cheeseboards and so on. I want people to see each preserve not as one dimensional, but as something with vast possibilities. I've made this my mission, collaborating with other cooks and chefs, running pop-ups and writing recipes to spread this idea.

If you've come this far, you've probably already made your own preserves, or just love preserves and collect many, but now may have the dilemma of surplus jars of things. You can only gift so many, and with modern fridges and freezers, we take our food's endurance for granted and let it sit, only to buy more. I call this the "condiment ghost-town".

Every time you look in your fridge and you see a condiment ghost-town growing, you can refer to these recipes for fresh ideas. But also, when you bring home a new condiment and are at a loss for ideas on how to eat it, these pages should help.

This book is made up of sections dedicated to different types of preserves. Alongside each preserve recipe, I've also included two to three recipes that use that preserve as an ingredient. The recipe combinations are suggestions and include notes for alternatives – and they are open to interpretation if you want to experiment. Many of the recipes are influenced by the country where the preserve originates, but make no claim to authenticity.

One person's "finely chopped" is another's "roughly chopped", just as one person's centimetre can be another's inch. But size really does matter when it comes to the way food breaks down when cooking, so do try to follow my instructions if you want the recipes to work as intended. The equipment you use is important, too: copper, steel or cast iron; little or large; gas or induction; even the weather on the day can affect your results, especially when making jam. The key is to practise and persevere.

When it comes to cooking, I'm a big believer in trusting your senses. Recipes passed down through the oral tradition don't come with a set of measurements and instructions, more instincts and feelings. In my Nan's scone recipe (page 197), I quote my Auntie Cher talking about how her mother didn't have a recipe for her scones, as they were always made on look and feel. I don't just cook with my hands and eyes – I also use my ears, nose and mouth. Let all of your senses guide you. Listen to the change in a sizzle or bubble; smell when the caramel has turned and burned; feel the heat that comes from a barbecue; and taste, taste, taste as you cook – seasoning is subjective but essential.

A final but invaluable word of advice: always read the recipe in full before you start cooking it. Like any good book, recipes often have plot twists. Many refer to other recipes elsewhere in the book for the full story. In this book the intention is to utilize your condiment

ghost-town. This is a key part of making your cooking more sustainable and learning to cook from scratch. Use store-bought products like ricotta, tortillas, bread and custard wherever you choose to, but you'll be surprised by how easily you can make these yourself, with less effort than you might have imagined. Give it a go - the custard (page 206) and ice cream (page 135) are both game-changers.

Main tips

- Follow the seasons.
- Produce should always be fresh and free-range, organic if you can.
- Learn from your mistakes - take notes and enjoy the process.
- Befriend your local butcher, fishmonger, greengrocer - they can advise you on what's at its best.
- Things don't have to be expensive to be good quality - make conscious decisions with your spending power.

Pickle

Brine pickling

The beauty of pickling is that you can experiment with almost everything. It's the simplest, quickest way of preserving the seasonal glut and a great place to start your preserving journey. The following chapter offers you some easy pickling recipes. The main premise is to completely submerge fruit or vegetables in a brine made from vinegar, salt and sugar (and spices, for extra flavour).

There are three typical ways to create a pickle:

Quick pickles

These are the sweetest of pickles, the higher sugar content making them immediately palatable. Generally, this is what you are served in restaurants. These pickles are not made for longevity and will start to ferment in their containers if left out and not stored correctly over time. They need to be eaten promptly and kept in the fridge.

Preserving pickles

Preserved pickles are created for longevity and need time to mellow in a jar (usually three to four weeks) so that the vinegars, sugars and spices gradually relax in their sharpness and become more palatable. For these you need to use high acetic acid vinegars (of over 5% acidity), and this high acidity creates a sort of time capsule for a fruit or vegetable to last longer without exposure to air. They can be stored in a dark cupboard for 12-24 months and only need refrigeration once they have been opened.

Fermented pickles

These let produce go through the fermentation process (page 58), creating a stabilized brine for them to "live" in without decomposing. They don't use a vinegar brine, rather they break down naturally in salted water. These generally take two to six weeks to ferment, depending on what you are preserving, and need to be refrigerated thereafter to slow the fermentation process and prevent the produce from becoming too soft or over-fermented in the jar.

Produce

Use fresh seasonal fruit and vegetables that are firm to the touch. The point of pickling is to preserve how the produce is now, at its best. Keep your aging fruit and vegetables for chutneys and sauces – a process in which you reduce and render down (where freshness is less essential).

Porosity is an important feature in pickling and will affect the process. For example, cucumbers are porous and can become soft, so you can salt them for a few hours, to draw out excess moisture, and then rinse and dry them before jarring. Harder produce, such as beetroot (beets), firm peaches or pears, is less porous and may need to be blanched for one to two minutes before pickling, to allow the brine to penetrate. Some fruits, like cherries or plums, can be pricked or stoned (pitted) to better absorb the brine.

Always wash and prep your produce before pickling, then hull, chop, slice, dice, wedge, prick, peel, blanch. I always like to think how I want to present or eat the pickle later to determine how I should prep a fruit or vegetable.

Vinegars

Vinegars are themselves ferments. Cider vinegar is made from apples, red and white wine vinegar originally from grapes, malt and rice vinegar from grains. These ingredients have already gone through the natural process of breaking down to become vinegars, therefore creating the perfect sterile environment for pickling something else.

When choosing a vinegar for a pickle's longevity, make sure you are using one with acid levels of 5% and over (this will be written on the bottle). Some vinegars are naturally lower in acidity than others. For example, rice wine vinegar is best kept for your quick pickles; its lower acidity makes it quickly palatable, but this lesser potency means it won't preserve your produce.

Avoid using homemade vinegars for pickles made for longevity. You won't know the acidity level, so these should be kept for salad dressings and quick pickles.

Sugars

These are used to balance the sharpness of the vinegar. Use golden or white caster or granulated sugar to balance the vinegar when making your brines. Experiment with different sugars, keeping in mind that some of the darker ones may dominate the flavour. If you want to experiment with a raw honey, be aware that it is an active ingredient and could encourage fermentation in the jar – which you don't always want.

Salt

This is used for preservation and taste but can also be used to extract liquid from vegetables, keeping them crunchy (as is the case with pickled cucumbers and courgettes/zucchini). Salt is one of the oldest methods for preserving, providing an unfriendly environment for yeasts, bacteria and moulds to thrive in. Avoid using iodized salts, as sometimes they have additives that hinder a pickle's sterile environment. Sea salt is your best option for its natural purity.

Spices (and co)

Experiment with flavour profiles. Match what you think goes well together and start collecting a variety to play around with. Here are some suggestions for flavour pairings:

With vegetables:
Dried (whole, seeds or ground): coriander, fennel, cumin, cloves, cinnamon, peppercorns (black, pink and white), mace, saffron, cardamom (green and black), mustard (yellow and brown), turmeric, juniper berries, bay leaves, chillies (chilli powders/flakes)
Fresh: ginger, chillies, garlic, citrus fruit (zest/rind/juice), mint, basil, sage, thyme, rosemary, bay leaves, lemon thyme, lemon verbena

With fruit:
Dried (whole, seeds or ground): star anise, cardamom (green and black), fennel, cloves, cinnamon, nutmeg, peppercorns (black, pink and white), mustard (yellow), juniper berries, bay leaves, chilli (red pepper) flakes, mace, saffron
Fresh: ginger, chillies, citrus fruit (zest/rind/juice), mint, basil, rosemary, lemon thyme, lemon verbena, sage, hibiscus, lavender, chamomile, rose

Equipment

- Jars with lids – new or used (providing any recycled ones don't have chips or cracks, and the rubber seals in the lids are still intact)
- Food-grade Tupperware for quick pickles
- A large saucepan (avoid aluminium or copper as the vinegars react to these metals)
- A measuring jug (cup)
- Wide-mouthed funnels
- A chopstick
- If you really want to, you can also get a pH thermometer or pH strips to test whether your pickles have the correct acid levels for longevity, but these are not essential.

Vinegar brine process

Referring to your individual recipe for quantities, combine vinegar, water, sugar, salt and spices in a large, non-reactive pan, keeping any fresh herbs or garlic cloves to one side until the jarring stage. Place over a medium heat, stirring until the sugar and salt dissolve and the spices infuse. Bring to the boil and simmer for 5 minutes, then allow the brine to cool slightly (or completely if using more porous produce, such as cucumber).

Pack your prepped produce into appropriately sized, clean (or sterilized - page 212), cool jars. Try to fit in as much as possible without squashing or forcing too tightly, leaving a gap of about 1cm (½in) from the top rim.

Pour the brine over the fruit or veg. Gently tap out any trapped bubbles, or use a chopstick to manoeuvre the bubbles out, making sure you get out as many as you can (this trapped air can encourage fermentation). Top up with brine again so the produce is entirely covered, up to 2-3mm (⅛in) from the very top, and seal with a sterilized dry lid.

Some preservers use a canning bath or heat process after sealing, where the jars are brought to a gentle boil in a bath of water covering them entirely for 10-15 minutes. This can add to the longevity of your preserves and ensure a secure seal, but it can also cook the produce, making it mushier. I always think vinegar and salt should be enough for longevity, as they create a sterile environment where unwanted bacteria don't choose to reside, so I tend not to "can" my pickles.

Troubleshooting

Not enough brine? This can happen because vegetables come in different sizes and different cooks cut them in different ways. The shape of the jar can affect things, too. If you find yourself just a couple of millimetres out, then top up with a little vinegar. However, if you find yourself with anything above 40ml (3 tablespoons) too little, it's best to make some more. It is better to have too much brine with some left over, which you can always store in the fridge and use to pickle something else.

Always store pickles in a cool, dark place. If your pickles are stored somewhere warm, they could start to ferment in their jars. These are still edible, and sometimes even more delicious, so don't be afraid if a pickle starts to bubble and fizz over when opened. Just store it in the fridge thereafter.

Cloudy white sediment that resembles mould is also perfectly fine. This is usually iodine, which results from using table salt. For this reason, I prefer to use pure sea salt for pickling. Table salt can also develop yeasts, which will encourage fermentation.

To keep vegetables from going too soft, a good trick is to cut and salt them for 3-6 hours, then wash this salt off completely, pat dry and then jar. This will keep them crunchy and crisp. Another trick is to add a tannic leaf to the top of the jar: grape leaves, oat leaves, raspberry or fresh bay leaves, or you can even try whole tea leaves.

Vinegar brine pickled vegetables

Almost all vegetables can be pickled with a spiced vinegar brine, although I generally stay away from starchy vegetables (that said, I have eaten pickled potatoes in restaurants). Restaurant pickle brines often differ from preserving pickle brines. Chefs tend to pickle for a day and up to a week, making a "quick pickle". These pickles work on a 3:2:1 ratio of vinegar:water:sugar. This extra water and sugar makes it palatable quicker compared to a "preserving pickle" where the higher acidity from the extra vinegar creates longevity.

Opposite are two brine recipes for these two types of pickle, plus some of my favourite pickled vegetable recipes. The sugar and salt contents change to adapt to the type of vegetable used, tweaked according to how sweet the produce is naturally. Try mixing and matching different spices with vinegars or omitting any added water and replacing it with distilled alcohols.

Peel, slice, dice, cut, disc, baton and grate your vegetables as you wish them to be presented on your plate. Think about the absorbency of the vegetables, as this can determine the thickness of your cut. Some, like cucumber, shouldn't be cut too thin as they can turn soft and mushy.

Preserving pickle brine

Makes about 850ml (3½ cups), enough for a 1 litre (34fl oz) jar

650ml (2¾ cups) vinegar
150ml (⅔ cup) filtered water
50–80g (¼–generous ⅓ cup) sugar
3–10g (½–2 tsp) sea salt
spices/herbs, as desired

Quick pickle brine, 3:2:1

Makes about 450ml (scant 2 cups)

240ml (1 cup) vinegar
160ml (⅔ cup) filtered water
80g (generous ⅓ cup) sugar
pinch of sea salt (optional)
spices/herbs, as desired

Pickled beetroot

Makes a 750ml (25fl oz) jar

450–500g (1lb–1lb 2oz) beetroot
    (beets), peeled, thinly sliced/
    diced (blanched in boiling water)
    or grated
450ml (scant 2 cups) white wine
    vinegar
100ml (⅓ cup) filtered water
50g (¼ cup) white sugar
1 tsp sea salt
1 tsp black peppercorns
2 bay leaves
8 cloves, gently toasted
3 green cardamom pods, gently
    smashed
2–3 pared strips of lemon zest

Pickled onions/silverskins

Makes a 500ml (17fl oz) jar

250g (9oz) pickling onions/
    silverskins, blanched and peeled
240ml (1 cup) distilled malt vinegar
80ml (5 Tbsp) filtered water
50g (¼ cup) white sugar
1½ tsp sea salt
1 tsp chilli (red pepper) flakes
¾ tsp coriander seeds
¾ tsp mustard seeds
¾ tsp fennel seeds
¾ tsp black peppercorns

Pickled peppers

Makes a 1 litre (34fl oz) jar

3–4 Romano peppers, whole and
    pricked or cut to fit jar
600ml (2½ cups) white wine vinegar
100ml (⅓ cup) filtered water
60g (5 Tbsp) white sugar
2 tsp sea salt
3 bay leaves
2 tsp coriander seeds
2 tsp black peppercorns
2 tsp juniper berries
2 garlic cloves, peeled, whole
    or chopped

Citrus-pickled fennel

Makes a 1 litre (34fl oz) jar

1 large or 2 medium fennel bulb/s, thinly
  sliced, halved or cut into wedges
350ml (1½ cups) white wine vinegar
150ml (⅔ cup) filtered water
30g (2½ Tbsp) white sugar
1 tsp sea salt
zest (in fine strips) of 1 orange
zest (in fine strips) of 1 lemon
zest (in fine strips) of 1 lime
½ tsp fennel seeds
½ tsp black peppercorns
½ tsp chilli (red pepper) flakes

Pickled jalapeños

Makes a 500ml (17fl oz) jar

200g (7oz) jalapeños, sliced into discs
  3–5mm (⅛–¼in) thick
250ml (1 cup) cider vinegar
200ml (¾ cup) filtered water
40g (3¼ Tbsp) white/golden
  granulated sugar
1 tsp sea salt
1 tsp black peppercorns
1 tsp cumin seeds
1 garlic clove, peeled
1 bay leaf

Pickled radish/mooli

Makes a 500ml (17fl oz) jar

225g (8oz) radishes, thinly sliced into
  discs, quartered or pricked whole
  or 1 medium mooli, thinly sliced,
  ribboned or cut into batons
240ml (1 cup) cider vinegar
80ml (5 Tbsp) filtered water
40g (3¼ Tbsp) white/golden
  granulated sugar
1 tsp sea salt
1 tsp black peppercorns
½ tsp mustard seeds
2 bay leaves
finely grated zest of ½ lime
juice of 1 lime
1 bird's-eye chilli, halved (optional)

Whisky-pickled carrot

Makes a 1 litre (34fl oz) jar

600g (1lb 5oz) carrots, peeled, cut
  into batons or discs, or grated
650ml (2¾ cups) cider vinegar
70ml (5 Tbsp) filtered water
50ml (3½ Tbsp) whisky
50g (¼ cup) white sugar
20g (4 tsp) sea salt
zest and juice of 1 orange
3 tsp chilli (red pepper) flakes
2 tsp black peppercorns

Pea and mint pickle

Makes a 750ml (25fl oz) jar

500g (1lb 2oz) fresh peas
  (podded weight)
350ml (1½ cups) cider vinegar
80ml (5 Tbsp) filtered water
30g (2½ Tbsp) white sugar
1½ tsp sea salt
1–2 bird's-eye chillies, roughly
  chopped
1 tsp black peppercorns
6–8 fresh mint leaves

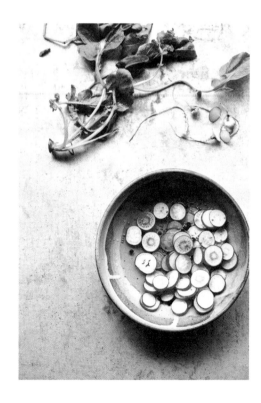

Notes
- The method for making up each brine is the same, although you can experiment with different spice and vinegar combinations. Follow the instructions on page 15.
- Quick pickles can be put into any sealed airtight container – ensure the produce is completely covered by the brine – and stored in the fridge. They will be ready to eat in 1–2 hours. Use within 2–4 weeks.
- The preserved pickles will need to be stored unopened in a cool, dark place for about 3–4 weeks before opening. Once opened, store in the fridge for greater longevity.
- Different vegetables differ in freshness over time, generally 6–18 months, so keep an eye on them and open a test jar to try.

Kiwi burger with pickled beetroot and a fried egg

New Zealanders like to put beetroot (beets) and a fried egg into a burger. When I was a kid, we would get fish'n'chips every Friday night from the local fish'n'chip shop - there was one in every neighbourhood. This is where you could buy such "Kiwi" burgers, along with battered fish burgers, paua fritters (a type of abalone) and battered deep-fried oysters. The burgers were stacked high with an abundance of ingredients: lettuce, beetroot, eggs and sometimes even pineapple. These early experiences informed my philosophy on food. Whether it be fast or slow food, the ingredients should be fresh, seasonal and well sourced.

Makes 4 burgers

400g (14oz) minced (ground) beef (good quality, locally sourced), at room temperature
4 Tbsp rapeseed (canola) or sunflower oil (or 3 Tbsp oil and 1 Tbsp butter)
1 large red onion, finely sliced into discs or semi-circles
4 very thin slices of Emmental, Gouda or Jarlsberg cheese
4 free-range eggs
4 burger buns, or brioche/milk buns (Homemade, page 198)
4 Tbsp tomato ketchup or tomato chutney
4 Tbsp Dijon or wholegrain mustard
1-2 large tomatoes, sliced
8-12 slices of Pickled Beetroot (page 17)
4 large iceberg or round lettuce leaves
sea salt and freshly ground black pepper

Divide the meat into 4 equal amounts and roll each into a ball. Sandwich each ball between 2 pieces of baking paper, and using a rolling pin, roll them out into patties about 1cm (½in) smaller than your burger buns. Set aside.

Heat 3 tablespoons of the oil in a large frying pan over a medium–high heat. Add the onions and fry for 5–6 minutes, until soft and a little charred. Remove from the pan and set aside. Keeping a medium–high heat, add the patties, two at a time. Generously season with salt and pepper. Cook for 30 seconds, then gently squash the patties down with a fish slice to the diameter of your burger buns and cook for a further 1½ minutes. Flip the patties, season again, and place a slice of cheese on top of each patty so it gently hugs when melted. Cook for 1 minute for medium rare, or 2 minutes for medium. Remove the patties and set aside to rest while you cook the next batch.

Meanwhile, in a separate frying pan, fry your eggs with the remaining tablespoon of oil – see page 76 for instructions.

When the patties are cooked, gently toast the burger buns in the same pan, pressing the sliced sides into the pan for 20–30 seconds.

To stack your burgers, spread ketchup on the bottom buns and mustard on the tops. Place each cheese-coated patty on a bottom bun, then top with the fried egg, 1–3 slices of tomato, 2–3 slices of pickled beetroot, lettuce and lastly some of the fried onions, before finishing with the bun tops.

Note
- Some New Zealanders will say it's not a Kiwi burger without a pineapple
  ring. If you want to try this sweeter version, char some pineapple slices
  in a griddle pan or under the grill (broiler) and add to the stack in place
  of the tomato.

Spicy sweet pickled carrot salad with toasted peanuts

This salad is very versatile and seems to have an international passport as it complements dishes from around the world. See the notes below for ideas on what to match it with.

Serves 2–4

300ml (1¼ cups) Quick Pickle Brine, 3:2:1 (page 17), using cider vinegar and spiced with juice of ½ lime, ½ tsp black peppercorns, ½ lemongrass stalk, 1 tsp chilli (red pepper) flakes, 1 cinnamon stick and 1 star anise
400g (14oz) carrots, grated or finely julienned
1½ tsp light cooking oil
1 small garlic clove, finely chopped
2cm (¾in) piece of fresh root ginger, finely grated
juice of ½ lime
1 Tbsp fish sauce
35g (3 Tbsp) palm sugar or caster or granulated sugar
30–40g (¼ cup) unsalted peanuts, roughly chopped
bunch of mint, roughly chopped
bunch of coriander (cilantro), roughly chopped
1–2 hot red chillies (Thai/bird's-eye are best), sliced lengthways (optional)
1 Tbsp sesame oil

The day before, or at least 1–2 hours ahead, make your quick pickled carrot. Place the carrots in a small bowl and pour over the cooled brine to completely cover them. Weight the carrots down under the brine, cover and leave to pickle (refrigerate if leaving overnight).

The next day, or when ready to cook, drain the carrots in a colander set over a bowl, reserving the brine. Scoop out the spices.

Heat the oil in a saucepan over a medium heat along with the garlic and ginger. When it starts to sizzle, cook for 30 seconds. Measure out 100ml (generous ⅓ cup) of the reserved brine and add to the pan. Add the lime juice, fish sauce and sugar. Bring to a rapid boil, then reduce the heat to a low simmer for 5–7 minutes, until the liquid has reduced and resembles a light syrup. Leave to cool to room temperature.

Meanwhile, lightly toast the peanuts in a small dry frying pan.

Put the drained carrots into a large bowl, toss with the herbs, chillies and peanuts and pour over your cooled brine dressing. Cover and chill in the fridge for at least 30 minutes.

Serve drizzled with sesame oil.

Notes
- Deseed the chillies if you like less heat.
- Serve alongside a Thai red or green curry, or on vermicelli rice noodles with spiced grilled (broiled) chicken or prawns (shrimp), or simply on sticky coconut jasmine rice.
- Bulk it up by adding shredded cabbage to make a Thai slaw salad.
- Match with a jackfruit or Indian chicken curry, with homemade chapattis and a mint raita.
- Great with Moroccan spiced shredded lamb, or a vegetarian tagine with labneh and flatbread.
- Stuff into a baguette with spicy pork or crispy tofu to make a Vietnamese *banh mi.*

Whey potato salad with pickled peas and mint

Whey is such a fantastic by-product ingredient to work with – it adds a creamy depth of flavour to new potatoes when you boil them in it.

I like potato salad for its creaminess; it seems to me to be the most indulgent of all the salads. Here, the pickled peas add a bit of a punch to cut through all of the indulgence. This recipe is an upgraded version of the classic salad we've seen at many a dinner party or barbecue over the years – retro, but we will always be friends.

Serves 2–3

600g (1lb 5oz) baby new potatoes or baby Jersey royals, washed and cut to the same size as the smallest
500ml (2 cups) Whey (page 204) or water
2 strips of streaky bacon (optional)
50–60g (2oz) Pea and Mint Pickle (page 18)
2–3 Tbsp mayonnaise (Homemade, page 203)
8–10 mint leaves, roughly torn
sea salt and freshly ground black pepper

Place the potatoes in a large saucepan along with a pinch of sea salt and the whey (or water) and bring to the boil. Boil for 10–12 minutes, until just soft to the tip of a sharp knife. Drain and transfer to a large bowl to cool to room temperature. There will be a cheesy by-product from the hard boiling in whey – it doesn't matter if some of this makes it into your salad.

Meanwhile, fry the bacon, if using, in a hot pan, or grill (broil) it until crispy. Drain on paper towels. Once cool, remove the rind and roughly chop. Add to the potatoes and mix through.

Spoon out your pickled peas with a slotted spoon, picking out any hard spices you might not want to bite down on, and mix through the potatoes. Season generously with pepper, then gently fold through the mayonnaise and mint leaves. Taste and season again with salt and pepper, if needed.

Notes
- Substitute the pickled peas for chopped-up gherkins, capers or pickled radishes. Or be daring and try pickled grapes.
- This works equally well with lightly braised peas (we all have these in our freezer).
- Try using the homemade Pickle-brine Mayonnaise (page 203) using the brine from the peas or pickled radishes, matching the flavours that you've used in the salad.

Pickled pea frittata

I love to share what I've learnt in preserving, so I teach my skills to others. I feel that in addition to teaching how to pickle or ferment there is also a lesson in the ethics that surround food preservation, our relationship to food, where it comes from and how to actually engage in using/eating your preserves. One Sunday a month, I hold an intensive, six-hour class where I cook lunch, each dish incorporating some type of preserve. This frittata is a common occurrence in these classes, served with a freshly made chutney from that day, thereby incorporating a pickle and a chutney into an everyday meal.

Serves 8–10

1½ Tbsp unsalted butter
2 Tbsp light olive oil, or rapeseed
  (canola) or vegetable oil
2 large onions, diced
200g (7oz) Pea and Mint Pickle
  (page 18)
120g (4½oz) mixed fresh herbs (mint,
  flat-leaf parsley, basil, coriander
  [cilantro], chives), roughly
  chopped
12 large free-range eggs, whisked
sea salt and freshly ground black
  pepper, to taste

Preheat the oven to 200°C (180°C fan/400°F/gas mark 6), placing a rack in the grill (broil) position.

Warm the butter and oil in a large non-stick, oven-safe frying pan (about 26–28cm/10–11in) over a medium heat. Add the onions, season generously with salt and pepper, and cook the onions for 10–15 minutes, stirring until they are caramelized, glossy, sticky and sweet.

Reduce the heat slightly, add the pickled peas and cook for about 30 seconds, then stir through the herbs and arrange the ingredients equally around the pan. Pour in the whisked eggs and use a wooden spoon to move the ingredients around to distribute everything evenly. Cook for 5–6 minutes until the egg starts to set on the bottom of the frittata. Run a spatula around the edge of the frittata for ease of flipping it out later.

Switch the oven to grilling (broiling) and slide the frittata pan onto the rack. Cook with the oven door closed for a further 4–5 minutes, or until the top of the frittata is golden brown and it has cooked through.

Remove the pan from the oven and allow to cool slightly, then carefully flip the frittata onto a large board or plate. Sandwich another plate on top of the frittata and flip again, so that you have the pretty golden side facing up.

Slice into 8–10 wedges and serve with a chutney of your choice, if you like.

Notes
- If you only have a smaller pan or are cooking for just one or two people, you can reduce this recipe to make 4–6 slices. Use 8 eggs and reduce the cooking time to 4–5 minutes followed by 3–4 minutes to finish the top.
- Substitute the pickled peas for pickled carrots, pickled peppers, pickled fennel or pickled corn kernels.
- Add crumbled feta, goats' cheese or ricotta, or slice some cherry tomatoes in half and gently push into the top of the frittata while it is cooking on the stove top.

Notes
- Use pickled radish, pickled carrot or pickled red (bell) peppers as a substitute for the beetroot. Or if you find you don't have any of these pickles in stock, just add any of your favourite vegetables to the roasting pan instead.
- You can also try this salad without the butternut squash and shred some grilled (broiled) salmon or trout through instead – mix it up a bit.

Roast butternut, pickled beetroot, feta and Puy lentil salad

Sometimes, it's simplicity I crave. Simple flavour combinations to get me through the day. I love hearty root vegetables, and for a healthier take on comfort food Puy lentils are my go-to. This may be a common go-to for you, too: roasted beetroot and squash, a bit of creamy feta chucked in for good measure, rocket (arugula) for a peppery punch… However, this time try it with a sharp twist to the plot and add the pickled beetroot you made up weeks ago. It doesn't even need a dressing, just a squeeze of lemon, a drizzle of quality olive oil and a good season with salt and pepper. You'll end up adding pickled beetroot to all your salads.

Serves 2–4

300g (1½ cups) Puy lentils, or green speckled lentils, rinsed
600ml (2½ cups) vegetable stock
500g (1lb 2oz) butternut squash, skin on, cut into wedges 2cm (¾in) thick
3 Tbsp light olive oil, or rapeseed (canola) or vegetable oil
1 large red onion, cut into thick wedges
60g (2oz) Pickled Beetroot (page 17), cut into wedges/chunks
60g (2oz) feta cheese, crumbled
30–40g (1–1½oz) rocket (arugula) leaves, or fresh tarragon leaves
juice of 1 lemon
about 3 Tbsp good-quality extra-virgin olive oil
2 heaped Tbsp pumpkin seeds, lightly toasted
sea salt and freshly ground black pepper, to taste

Preheat the oven to 200°C (180°C fan/400°F/gas mark 6).

Combine the lentils and stock in a large saucepan, cover with the lid, and bring to the boil over a medium-high heat. This should take 7–8 minutes. Reduce the heat and keep at a steady simmer with the lid ajar for 15–20 minutes. Remove the lid for the last 5 minutes of cooking time to evaporate the remaining water. The lentils should be cooked but with a slight bite, so test them along the way – you don't want mushy lentils in the salad.

Meanwhile, place the butternut squash in a large roasting pan and drizzle over the light olive oil. Season generously with salt and pepper and use your hands to toss, coating the squash evenly. Bake in the middle of the oven for 8–10 minutes.

Remove the squash from the oven and turn the pieces over, then toss in the onion wedges, coating them with some of the cooking oils. Bake for a further 10–12 minutes or until cooked.

Remove the squash and onions from the oven and let rest for 6–7 minutes. If necessary, drain any excess water from the cooked lentils then gently toss them through the baked vegetables. Toss through the pickled beetroot, feta and rocket. Serve on a large plate, drizzled with the lemon juice and extra virgin olive oil and sprinkled with the toasted pumpkin seeds.

Smoked trout salad with pickled radish, ruby grapefruit and almonds

I first smoked fish with my dad in New Plymouth, New Zealand, about 15 years ago. I was visiting from London and we had been shopping at a bargain department store called "The Warehouse" where we came across a small, domestic, outdoor smoker. We decided to give it a go. My dad lives for the sea. As a fisherman, fishing is in his heart and if he could be out on a boat every morning at 4am, he would. So, fishing is in my blood and I have lots of blissful memories (and some rather nausea-tainted ones) of being out at sea with him on his fishing boat. It makes you more aware of what you eat when you have hunted and gathered it yourself.

Serves 2–4

1½ tsp white balsamic vinegar, or rice wine vinegar or sherry vinegar
1½ Tbsp extra-virgin olive oil
½ tsp honey
½ tsp wholegrain mustard
80g (3oz) baby leaf watercress, lamb's lettuce or pea shoots
2 fillets of smoked trout (250–350g/ 9–12oz) (Homemade, page 209)
4–6 Pickled Radishes (page 18), sliced
3–4 ruby grapefruit segments, cut into 1–2cm (½–¾in) cubes
20g (¼ cup) flaked (slivered) almonds, lightly toasted
sea salt and freshly ground black pepper, to taste

In a large bowl, make a dressing by whisking together the vinegar, olive oil, honey and mustard until it becomes lighter in appearance. Lightly season with salt and pepper. Add the watercress and toss with your hands so that the dressing coats all the leaves.

Break up the smoked trout in your hands into long strips. Place the pickled radishes on some paper towels and pat dry.

To serve, dress one large or 2–4 individual plates with a generous handful of watercress, equally distributing pieces of grapefruit and trout among them. Sprinkle over the radish slices and toasted almonds and season again, to taste, if necessary.

Notes
- Make this a "for all seasons" salad by mixing it up and using pickled beetroot, omitting the grapefruit and adding some crumbled feta.
- Try pickled fruit such as grapes or blackberries, once again taking out the grapefruit, and exchanging the almonds for lightly toasted hazelnuts or walnuts.
- If you can't get trout, then smoked salmon makes for a nice change. Try it cured (page 209) if you're not inclined to smokier flavours.

Notes
- The finer the grain the better the texture of the finished cornbread. Try blitzing the polenta, if yours is "coarse ground", in a food processor until very finely ground.
- Chopped chives and red onion, or charred sweetcorn and spring onions (scallions) work well in place of the jalapeños.
- If you don't have a cast-iron skillet, grease and line a deep 30 x 20cm (12 x 8in) baking pan with butter, pour the batter in and bake.

Whey cornbread with jalapeños

I used to share my kitchen in Hackney with the Portuguese pastry chef Diana Neto, who has won awards for her *pasteis de nata*. She also cooks the most mouth-watering buttermilk cornbread, and the smells that came from her side of the kitchen inspired me to make my own cornbread to use up the whey I had left over from making cheese (page 204). Diana would use chives, cheese and red onion in her cornbread, but I wanted to incorporate the spicy pickled jalapeños we were producing at Newton & Pott. Drizzle on a bit of honey and it takes anyone to Mexico.

Serves 6–8

400ml (1¾ cups) whey, buttermilk or 300ml (1¼ cups) plain yoghurt mixed with 150ml (⅔ cup) milk
100g (7 Tbsp) unsalted butter
160g (1 cup) fine corn (maize) flour/ fine cornmeal/very fine polenta
140g (generous 1 cup) plain (all-purpose) flour
1½ tsp baking powder
¼ tsp bicarbonate of soda (baking soda)
½ tsp sea salt
20g (5 tsp) light brown sugar
20g (1 heaped Tbsp) runny honey, plus extra for drizzling
1 large free-range egg, at room temperature, whisked
80–90g (3oz) Pickled Jalapeños (page 18), drained and patted dry, then half roughly chopped and half sliced

If using whey or buttermilk, let it stand at room temperature for at least 20 minutes to thicken slightly. If using yoghurt/milk mix, remove from the fridge 5–10 minutes before using.

Preheat the oven to 200°C (180°C fan/400°F/gas mark 6).

In a small saucepan, melt 60g (4 tablespoons) of the butter and allow to cool.

Mix the corn flour/cornmeal/polenta, plain flour, baking powder, bicarbonate of soda and salt in a large bowl. In another bowl, whisk the melted butter with the sugar and honey until it becomes smooth and thick. Add the egg into the dry mixture until evenly incorporated, then fold in the whey (or buttermilk/ yoghurt). Add the roughly chopped jalapeños and finally stir through the sweetened butter mixture until just combined – don't overmix.

Melt the remaining 40g (3 tablespoons) of butter in a 14–20cm (5½–8in) cast-iron skillet over a medium-high heat, swirling the butter around so that it coats the bottom and sides of the pan. Pour the batter into the hot skillet and spread it with a spatula, levelling the top. Scatter over the jalapeño slices to decorate.

Transfer the skillet to the middle of the oven and bake for 30–35 minutes until the top of the cornbread is golden brown and an inserted skewer comes out clean.

Drizzle a couple of tablespoons of honey over the bread while it is still hot, then put the skillet on a wire rack and let cool for 3–5 minutes. Serve the still-hot bread in slices, although it is just as delicious when cold.

Tacos four ways with quick pickles and jalapeño mayonnaise

My obsession with Mexico started a long time ago, mostly because of the colourful representations I had seen of it in magazines and movies (before Instagram). So, when my husband asked me to marry him ten years ago, I said I would on one condition… could we go to Mexico on our honeymoon? Luckily, he said yes.

Mexican food shares this colourful reputation. It creates an uplifting feeling that's contagious. So, be vibrant and creative: mix it up, make two or all of the taco fillings below, or take bits from one and add to another. The idea is "food to be shared", to create a feeling of togetherness whether you're making it for a family of four, a group of friends or just for two. Allow yourself to come alive with the flavours, spices and colours.

Toppings

Quick pickled red cabbage	200g (7oz) red cabbage, very finely shredded; and 175ml (¾ cup) Quick Pickle Brine, 3:2:1 (page 17), using white wine vinegar and spiced with ½ tsp sea salt, ¼ tsp black peppercorns, ¼ tsp chilli (red pepper) flakes, ½ tsp mustard seeds, 1 bay leaf, juice of ½ lime
Quick pickled red onion	1 red onion, very finely sliced; and 100ml (generous ⅓ cup) Quick Pickle Brine, 3:2:1 (page 17), using red wine vinegar and spiced with ½ tsp sea salt, ¼ tsp black peppercorns, ¼ tsp chilli (red pepper) flakes, ½ tsp mustard seeds, 1 bay leaf, juice of ½ lime
Pickled jalapeño mayonnaise	60g (2oz) Pickled Jalapeños (page 18), roughly chopped; 2 Tbsp jalapeño pickle brine (from the jar); and 200–250g (about 1 cup) mayonnaise (Homemade, page 203)
Pickled jalapeño vegan mayo	30g (1oz) Pickled Jalapeños (page 18), roughly chopped; 1 Tbsp jalapeño pickle brine (from the jar); and 100–150g (about ½ cup) vegan mayo (Homemade, page 203)
Mango salsa	½ large mango, cut into 5mm–1cm (¼–½in) cubes; ½ red onion, finely diced (optional); ½ small red (bell) pepper, diced; a handful of coriander (cilantro), roughly chopped; juice of ½ lime and sea salt and freshly ground black pepper, to taste

Adobo-spiced grilled pork tacos

Serves 4–5

10g (⅓oz) dried chipotles (smoked
    jalapeños), Scotch bonnet or
    other smoky hot chillies
100ml (generous ⅓ cup) boiling
    water
4 garlic cloves, peeled
½ tsp dried oregano
½ tsp ground cinnamon
2 tsp smoked paprika (add extra
    ½ tsp if the chillies aren't smoky)
2 cloves
4 Tbsp apple cider vinegar
900g–1kg (2lb–2lb 4oz) boneless
    rolled and tied pork shoulder
10–12 corn tortillas (Homemade,
    page 200)
8–10 splashes of Tabasco sauce,
    or 5 bird's-eye chillies, roughly
    chopped
1 spring onion (scallion), sliced
sea salt and freshly ground black
    pepper, to taste

To serve
4–5 pineapple rings
Quick Pickled Red Onion (see
    Toppings)
handful of coriander (cilantro) leaves
Pickled Jalapeño Mayonnaise
    (see Toppings)

Cover the dried chillies with the boiling water and
leave to soak for 10–15 minutes. Drain and transfer
them to a food processor, add the garlic, oregano,
cinnamon, smoked paprika, cloves and vinegar and
blitz until smooth.

Using a very sharp knife, begin to cut the rolled pork
shoulder in half, through the middle between the
strings – you will need to stop before you cut all the
way through as you want the pieces to remain joined
at the bottom, opening out like the pages of a book.
Season both sides generously with salt and pepper,
then smother the meat with the chilli paste. Close
up the "book" again, place in a container, cover and
marinate in the fridge for at least 2 hours.

At least 30 minutes before cooking, remove the meat
from the fridge and open it out like a book. Preheat
the grill (broiler) to very high and place a rack one-
third of the way down from the top of the oven.

Place the meat on a baking tray under the grill and
grill for 20–30 minutes with the door ajar. Turn the
meat 4–6 times during cooking for an even char,
watching so the surface doesn't burn. This may
need more or less time according to your grill.

Meanwhile, make/prep the corn tortillas, wrap in a
dish towel and keep warm in the low oven until ready
to serve.

Remove the meat, sprinkle over the Tabasco sauce,
or chopped chillies, and spring onions, then grill for
a further 8–10 minutes until medium. Ideally, you are
aiming for the temperature inside the meat to be
63°C (145°F) minimum on a meat thermometer. Let
the pork rest for 10 minutes out of the oven before
slicing into strips.

Cook the pineapple rings either under the grill or in
a very hot griddle pan until charred with dark lines,
then chop into bite-sized pieces.

Serve everything on separate plates so people can
build their own tacos. I recommend stacking each
tortilla with pork, quick pickled onion, pineapple,
coriander and a drizzle of jalapeño mayo.

(continues)

Buttermilk fried chicken tacos

Serves 2–4

300–350g (10½–12oz) free-range
  skinless chicken thighs, cut into
  strips (approx. 2.5 x 8cm [1 x 3in])
300ml (1¼ cups) buttermilk
vegetable oil, for deep-frying
6–8 corn tortillas (Homemade, page
  200)
1 corn cob, husk removed
1 Tbsp olive oil
1 free-range egg, whisked
250g (3–4 cups) breadcrumbs
  (regular, panko or Homemade,
  page 199)
sea salt and freshly ground black
  pepper, to taste

To serve

1 avocado, flesh sliced
Quick Pickled Red Onion (see
  Toppings)
Pickled Jalapeño Mayonnaise
  (see Toppings)
zest of 1 lime
1–2 tsp smoked paprika

Season the chicken strips with salt and pepper and place in a bowl. Pour over the buttermilk, then cover and place in the fridge to marinate for 4–8 hours.

When ready to cook, preheat the grill (broiler) to high and the oven to very low. Heat enough oil for deep-frying in a large heavy-based saucepan or deep-fat fryer to 175°C (350°F).

Make/prep the corn tortillas, wrap in a dish towel and keep warm in the oven until ready to serve.

Rub the corn with the olive oil and season with salt and pepper. Grill (broil) for 4–6 minutes, turning every minute, until the corn is golden and charred in places. Remove and let cool, then slice off the corn kernels and place in a serving bowl.

With the egg and breadcrumbs in separate bowls, dip the chicken strips first into the egg and then into the breadcrumbs until completely covered.

Deep-fry the chicken strips in batches of 3–4 for 2 minutes until golden brown. Remove with a slotted spoon to drain on paper towels and keep warm in the low oven with the tortillas until ready to serve.

Serve everything on separate plates so people can build their own tacos. I recommend stacking each tortilla with chicken, avocado, corn, pickled red onion, jalapeño mayo, a little lime zest and a dusting of smoked paprika on top.

Crumbed fish tacos

Serves 2–4

250–300g (9–10½oz) skinless cod
  or haddock fillets, cut into strips
  (approx. 2.5 x 8cm [1 x 3in])
juice of ½ lime
zest and juice of ½ lemon
vegetable oil, for deep-frying
6–8 corn tortillas (Homemade, page
  200)
1 free-range egg, whisked
200g (2½–3 cups) breadcrumbs
  (regular, panko or Homemade,
  page 199)
sea salt and freshly ground black
  pepper, to taste

Place the strips of fish in a bowl, season with salt and pepper, and sprinkle over the citrus zest and juices. Cover and marinate in the fridge for 5–10 minutes.

When ready to cook, preheat the oven to very low. Heat enough oil for deep-frying in a large heavy-based saucepan or deep-fat fryer to 175°C (350°F).

Make/prep the corn tortillas, wrap in a dish towel and keep warm in the low oven until ready to serve.

With the egg and breadcrumbs in separate bowls, dip the fish strips first into the egg and then into the breadcrumbs until completely covered.

To serve
Pickled Jalapeño Mayonnaise
    (see Toppings)
Quick Pickled Red Cabbage
    (see Toppings)
handful of coriander (cilantro),
    leaves only
1 lime, cut into wedges

Deep-fry the coated fish strips in batches of
3–4 for 1–1½ minutes until golden brown. Remove
with a slotted spoon to drain on paper towels and
keep warm in the low oven with the tortillas until
ready to serve.

Serve everything on separate plates so people can
build their own tacos. I recommend stacking each
tortilla first with jalapeño mayo, then the fish, quick
pickled cabbage, coriander and a squeeze of lime.

Vegan pulled adobo jackfruit tacos

Serves 2–4

2 Tbsp olive oil
1 Tbsp tomato purée (paste)
2 Tbsp maple syrup or agave syrup
1 Tbsp chipotle adobo sauce, or 10g
    (⅓oz) dried chipotles soaked
    in 3 Tbsp boiling water for 30
    minutes, then blitzed into a paste
    with 1 tsp dried oregano
small pinch each of sea salt and
    freshly ground black pepper
½ cinnamon stick
½ tsp chilli powder
1 tsp smoked paprika
½ tsp cayenne pepper
400g (14oz) can of young jackfruit,
    drained and rinsed
6–8 corn tortillas (Homemade, page
    200)
2 Tbsp vegetable, rapeseed (canola)
    or sunflower oil, for cooking
1 banana shallot, finely diced
2 garlic cloves, finely chopped
100ml (generous ⅓ cup) hot vegan
    stock

To serve
Mango Salsa (see Toppings)
Quick Pickled Red Onion (see
    Toppings)
Pickled Jalapeño Vegan Mayo
    (see Toppings)

Make a marinade by mixing the olive oil, tomato purée,
maple syrup, chipotle adobo sauce, salt and pepper,
cinnamon stick, chilli powder, smoked paprika and
cayenne pepper in a large bowl. Add the jackfruit and
mix it to coat it with the paste. Cover and marinate in
the fridge for 8–24 hours.

When ready to cook, preheat the oven to very low.
Make/prep the corn tortillas, wrap in a dish towel
and keep warm in the low oven until ready to serve.

Heat the vegetable oil in a large frying pan over
a medium heat and sauté the shallot for about
2–3 minutes until soft and glossy. Add the garlic
and fry for 1 minute. Add the marinated jackfruit along
with the hot stock and cover with a lid. Increase the
heat a little and let simmer and soften for about
5 minutes. Remove the lid and fry over a lower heat
for a further 6–10 minutes, using a wooden spoon
or a fork to squash and separate the jackfruit, making
it resemble pulled meat. Keep stirring until the liquid
has evaporated.

Serve everything on separate plates so people
can build their own tacos. I recommend stacking
each tortilla with the jackfruit, mango salsa, quick
pickled red onion and a drizzle of pickled jalapeño
vegan mayo.

Notes
- If you are having problems getting dried chipotles, simply dry some
  jalapeños yourself in a very low oven for 8-10 hours, then smoke them over
  a very low heat using oak or hickory chips (page 209) for 10-15 minutes.
- Try making your own pickle brine mayonnaise (page 203) if you don't
  have jalapeños.

Vinegar brine pickled fruit

Fruit is great pickled and this needs to be celebrated more. Pickled fruits can be added to sweet or savoury dishes alike, from cakes to salads. In desserts, they take the sweet edge off a dish and bring a bit of sharpness to your palate. In savouries, you get the sweet from the fruit and sharpness from the vinegar: sweet, sour, bitter, salty – the perfect umami.

I tend to make the spiced vinegar brines of pickled fruits sweeter than those of vegetables, matching baking-type spices with the fruits. In turn, these brines end up being more syrupy and, once the fruit has macerated for a time, I have been known to add them to cocktails (much as you would a vinegar drinking shrub).

Below are two general recipes for a sweeter fruit pickling brine. Sugars and salt are tweaked according to the sweetness of the fruits. Play around with these to suit your tastes, and taste your brines while making them, adding things when needed. Fruit pickles generally don't keep as well as vegetable ones, so they tend to need to be stored in the fridge to preserve them better.

Keep your fruits whole (skin on and pricked) or peeled, sliced, diced, cut into discs or batons, or grated. Prep the fruit bearing in mind how you want to present them later.

Preserving sweet pickle brine

Makes 850ml (3½ cups), enough for a 1 litre (34fl oz) jar

600ml (2½ cups) vinegar
150–200ml (⅔–¾ cup) filtered water
100–200g (½–1 cup) sugar
1–3g (¼–½ tsp) sea salt
spices/herbs, as desired

Quick sweet pickle brine, 1:1:1

Makes about 250ml (1 cup)

100ml (generous ⅓ cup) vinegar
100ml (⅓ cup) filtered water
100g (½ cup) sugar
pinch of sea salt (optional)
spices/herbs, as desired

Pickled pears

Makes a 1 litre (34fl oz) jar

2–3 pears, whole, pricked, or peeled
    or chopped (blanch if very firm)
600ml (2½ cups) white wine vinegar
200ml (¾ cup) filtered water
150g (¾ cup) white/golden
    granulated sugar
pinch of sea salt
3 strips of pared lemon zest
50ml (3½ Tbsp) lemon juice
    (from about 2 lemons)
1 cinnamon stick
3 cardamom pods, gently smashed
¾ tsp black peppercorns
3 sprigs of lemon thyme

Pickled cherries

Makes a 500ml (17fl oz) jar

300g (10½oz) cherries, pricked
    or stoned (pitted)
250ml (1 cup) cider vinegar
100ml (⅓ cup) filtered water
150g (¾ cup) white/golden
    granulated sugar
pinch of sea salt
3 strips of pared orange zest
¼ tsp ground cinnamon
½ tsp mustard seeds
1 tsp black peppercorns
1 bay leaf
2 cardamom pods, gently smashed

Pickled rhubarb

Makes a 1 litre (34fl oz) jar

600g (1lb 5oz) rhubarb, cut into
    slices 2cm (¾in) thick or 8–10cm
    (3–4in) batons
500ml (2 cups) white wine vinegar
200ml (¾ cup) filtered water
100g (½ cup) white/golden
    granulated sugar
pinch of sea salt
2 sprigs of lemon thyme
1 tsp black peppercorns
4 strips of pared orange zest
5cm (2in) piece of fresh root ginger,
    sliced

Pickled gooseberries

Makes a 1 litre (34fl oz) jar

600g (1lb 5oz) gooseberries, topped
    and tailed
300ml (1¼ cups) white wine vinegar
200ml (¾ cup) filtered water
120g (scant ⅔ cup) white/golden
    granulated sugar
pinch of sea salt
1 tsp black peppercorns
1 tsp fennel seeds
⅛ tsp crushed chilli (red pepper)
    flakes
2 strips of pared lemon zest
juice of ½ lemon

Pickled peaches

Makes a 1 litre (34fl oz) jar

3–4 peaches, halved or quartered,
    stoned (pitted)
600ml (2½ cups) white wine vinegar
200ml (¾ cup) filtered water
100g (½ cup) white/golden
    granulated sugar
pinch of sea salt
½ cinnamon stick
1 tsp black peppercorns
½ tsp chilli (red pepper) flakes
2 bay leaves
5 strips of pared lemon zest

Pickled plums

Makes a 750ml (25fl oz) jar

450g (1lb) plums, whole, pricked
250ml (1 cup) cider vinegar
150ml (⅔ cup) filtered water
100g (½ cup) white/golden
    granulated sugar
pinch of sea salt
3 strips of pared lemon zest
3 cardamom pods, gently crushed
2 star anise
½ tsp black peppercorns

Pickled blackberries/ blueberries

Makes a 500ml (17fl oz) jar

400g (14oz) blackberries or
    blueberries
250ml (1 cup) white wine vinegar
100ml (⅓ cup) filtered water
80g (generous ⅓ cup) white/golden
    granulated sugar
pinch of sea salt
½ cinnamon stick
½ tsp black peppercorns
½ tsp juniper berries
1 tsp yellow mustard seeds
1 bay leaf
2 strips of pared lemon zest
2cm (¾in) piece of fresh root ginger,
    sliced

Notes
- The method for making up each brine is the same, although you can experiment with different spice and vinegar combinations. Follow the instructions on page 15.
- Quick fruit pickles should be put into a sealed airtight container, ensuring the produce is completely covered by the brine and stored in the fridge. They will be ready to eat in 1-2 hours and need to be eaten within 2-4 weeks.
- Preserved pickles will need to be stored unopened in a cool, dark place for about 3-4 weeks before opening. Once opened, store in the fridge for greater longevity. Pears, peaches and berries tend to need moving to the fridge earlier, but plums, rhubarb and cherries seem to hold out in a cool, dark space for quite a while.
- Different fruits will keep for different amounts of time, 3-18 months, so keep an eye on them, as they may be tempted to ferment and the jars may need burping (to release the gases) from time to time. It is perfectly fine for them to start to ferment and the brine may become bubbly and fizz over, so open over a sink.

Endive with Taleggio, pickled pear and a toasted almond crumb

This recipe is best with Taleggio cheese. Its melty, velvety creaminess has just the right strength of flavour to balance the bitterness of endive (chicory) and the sharp, sweet, sour notes of the pickle. It's a perfect umami. You can try it with other cheeses and nuts, such as Gorgonzola and walnuts, but it just isn't quite the same. So, if you can, get your hands on this oozy Italian treasure which is becoming more readily available – don't go for a substitute.

Serves 2

2 Tbsp unsalted butter
1 Tbsp olive oil
2–3 sprigs of fresh thyme
2–3 endive (depending on their size), halved lengthways
2 Tbsp flaked (slivered) almonds, chopped hazelnuts or pumpkin seeds
2 Tbsp sourdough or regular breadcrumbs (Homemade, page 199)
120–180g (4–6oz) Taleggio cheese (about 60g/2oz per endive)
½–1 Pickled Pear (page 39)
sea salt and freshly ground black pepper, to taste

Preheat the grill (broiler) to high and place a rack one-third of the way down from the top of the oven.

Heat 1 tablespoon of the butter together with the oil in a large non-stick, oven-safe, frying pan over a medium heat. Add the thyme and fry for about 30 seconds.

Place the endive, cut-sides down, into the pan and cook for 6–8 minutes until lightly caramelized. Turn them over, season with salt and pepper and add the remaining butter if needed. Cook for a further 6–8 minutes until the juices begin to release and they start to sizzle. Keep an eye on them and keep moving them in the pan until they turn almost translucent but haven't browned.

Meanwhile, toast the nuts or seeds in a small dry frying pan over a medium-low heat. As soon as they start to sizzle and release some moisture, add the breadcrumbs and toast both together until golden, tossing as you go.

Cut the cheese into thick long slices (enough for each endive half) and lay a slice on each cut side of the endive in the pan. Grill (broil) with the oven door ajar for 3–5 minutes or until the cheese has melted across the endive and is turning golden on the edges.

Set aside to cool slightly for 3–4 minutes while you slice the pickled pear into wafer-thin slices. Dress each plate with the endive and pear, season with some freshly cracked pepper and generously sprinkle over the almond crumb.

Note
- I have eaten this dish with other fruit pickles, so if you have others to hand, try pickled cherries, blackberries, grapes, plums or gooseberries. I have even made this using a quick pickle of beetroot (beet) stalks or with a side of radish leaves. Use up all the bits you have to hand, from root to leaf.

Chocolate and pickled pear frangipane tart with citrus crème fraîche

If you've made pickled pears, treat them as you might a poached pear. Dip the whole pear into melted chocolate or try classic combinations like this tart with a sharp fruity addition. The sour notes of the pickle make a delicious change to any ordinary pear and chocolate tart.

Serves 10–12

1–2 Pickled Pears (page 39), halved lengthways and patted dry with paper towel

Shortcrust pastry
200g (1½ cups) plain (all-purpose) flour, plus extra for dusting
90g (⅔ cup) icing (confectioners') sugar
3 Tbsp cocoa powder
pinch of sea salt
100g (scant ½ cup) cold unsalted butter, cubed, plus extra for greasing
1 egg, chilled
1–2 Tbsp ice-cold water (if needed)

Frangipane
100g (scant ½ cup) unsalted butter, cubed
80g (3oz) dark chocolate (at least 70 per cent cocoa solids), roughly chopped
3 Tbsp cocoa powder
2 large eggs, at room temperature
100g (½ cup) golden caster or granulated sugar
180g (1¾ cups) ground almonds

To serve
300g (scant 1½ cups) crème fraîche
finely grated zest and juice of 1 lemon

To make the pastry, sift the flour, icing sugar, cocoa and salt into a large bowl. Add the cold butter and rub the mixture between your fingers into fine crumbs. Mix through the egg until the mixture clumps together. Add a little ice-cold water if needed to bring together. Shape into a ball, place in an airtight container and refrigerate for 60 minutes or up to 24 hours.

Grease a 24cm (9½in) loose-bottomed tart pan. Roll the chilled pastry out between two pieces of greaseproof paper lightly dusted with flour to a disc 28–30cm (11–12in) in diameter and about 2mm (1⁄16in) thick. Carefully line the tart pan with the pastry, gently pushing it into the edges and grooves of the pan using a little excess pastry. Refrigerate for 30 minutes.

Preheat the oven to 180°C (160°C fan/350°F/gas mark 4).

To make the frangipane, melt the butter and chocolate in a small bowl set over a pan of simmering water, stirring until completely smooth. Remove from the heat, whisk through the cocoa powder and set aside to cool, but not harden. In a separate bowl, whisk together the eggs, then whisk in the sugar until pale and creamy. Fold this through the melted chocolate mixture until just combined, then gently mix through the ground almonds.

Remove the tart shell from the fridge and prick the base. Fill with the frangipane mixture, spreading evenly with a spatula. Slice the pears into wedges or carefully fan-cut the pear halves and decoratively press them into the surface of the tart. It will rise slightly when baked to envelope them.

Bake in the middle of the oven for 30–40 minutes so that the surface is firm and a toothpick comes out clean. Cool completely then remove from the pan.

Serve with crème fraîche mixed with lemon zest and juice.

Notes
- Try this recipe with pickled cherries, apricots, peaches, raspberries or blackberries. Alternatively, make the recipe without pickled fruit and use ripe or poached fruit.
- Make the pastry a week in advance and freeze. Defrost it in the fridge overnight before making the tart.

Note
- Substitutes that work well are pickled peaches, pickled blackberries or
  pickled grapes.

Pickled cherry salad with lamb's lettuce, ricotta and whey dressing

I love this salad. The clean flavours and textures are well balanced and nothing overpowers anything else. It also celebrates my waste-not-want-not ideals of using up stuff. Make the effort to make your own ricotta-style cheese – it only needs a few ingredients and takes minimal time and you end up with the wonderful by-product that is the whey. I use it in several recipes throughout this book, here as the dressing to this salad.

Serves 2–3

140–160g (⅔ cup) ricotta
(Homemade, page 204)
8–10 Pickled Cherries (page 39)
2 Tbsp Whey (page 204) or 1 Tbsp
plain yoghurt mixed with 1 Tbsp
water
2 Tbsp extra-virgin olive oil
½ tsp Dijon or wholegrain mustard
½ tsp honey
1 tsp lemon juice
80g (3oz) lamb's lettuce (corn salad),
pea shoots or baby watercress,
washed and dried
40g (⅓ cup) hazelnuts, lightly
toasted and roughly chopped
sea salt and freshly ground black
pepper, to taste

If you are making your own ricotta-style soft cheese, ensure you make it the day before or at least 2 hours before you start, remembering to keep and store the whey, too.

Pick out the pickled cherries from their brine and place in a sieve or on paper towels to dry for 10–12 minutes. If your cherries are pitted, chop each into quarters; if not, chop roughly around the stone.

In a small bowl, whisk together the whey, olive oil, mustard, honey and lemon juice, taste and season accordingly with salt and pepper.

Divide the lettuce leaves among serving plates or arrange on one large plate, then dress with a couple of spoonfuls of the dressing. Spoon on bits of the ricotta here and there. Sprinkle over the chopped cherries and toasted hazelnuts, then dress again with any remaining dressing. Season with a crack of freshly ground black pepper to taste and serve.

Notes
- Substitute the cherries for pickled blackberries, peaches, rhubarb or pear slices.
- If you don't have pickled fruit to hand this recipe also works with fresh fruit. Alternatively, add a teaspoon of jam between spooning it into the pan holes and omit the matcha for a jammy friand instead.
- If you don't have a friand pan, use a regular muffin pan or play around with different shaped baking pans. Ensure you fill each hole just over two-thirds full and, if larger, consider that baking times might be longer.

Pickled cherry and matcha friands

I'm not a trained chef or baker but my friend Henrietta Inman is an amazing pâtisserie chef who uses natural ancient grains and seasonal fruit and vegetables. I've collaborated with her several times and we created these fun, tasty friands for an afternoon tea we put on called "Infused". They were a massive hit and I've now become obsessed with pickled fruit in desserts and baking. I hope it will be a new discovery that you may become obsessed with, too.

Makes 20 small friands

160g (scant ¾ cup) unsalted butter, cubed, plus extra for greasing
50g (generous ⅓ cup) plain (all-purpose) flour, plus extra for dusting
150g (1 cup) icing (confectioners') sugar
7g (3½ tsp) matcha (Japanese green tea powder)
120g (1¼ cups) ground almonds
pinch of salt
finely grated zest of 1 lemon
4 large free-range egg whites
20 Pickled Cherries (page 39), patted dry with paper towels

Preheat the oven to 200°C (180°C fan/400°F/gas mark 6).

Grease a 20-hole friand pan with melted butter and lightly dust each hole with sifted flour, ensuring an even covering. Gently tap the pan upside-down to get rid of the excess flour and place the pan in the fridge.

Melt the butter in a small saucepan over a medium heat until it turns dark golden brown and smells rich and nutty. Remove from the heat and strain through a fine mesh strainer or piece of muslin (cheesecloth). Set aside and cool to room temperature while you make the batter.

Sift the flour, icing sugar and matcha into a large bowl and mix in the ground almonds, salt and lemon zest. In a separate bowl, whisk the egg whites gently for a few minutes until they are frothy and fluffy, but not stiff. Mix into the dry ingredients, stirring until completely combined. Finally, mix through the cool browned butter until smooth and glossy.

Take the friand pan out of the fridge and fill each hole just over two-thirds full with batter. Place a pickled cherry in the centre of each hole. Bake in the middle of the oven for 10 minutes, then reduce the oven temperate to 180°C (160°C fan/350°F/gas mark 4), turn the pan around in the oven and bake for a further 10 minutes until the friands have a small peak on top and a slight spring to the touch.

Cool for 10 minutes in the pan, then run a knife around the edges of the friands to ease their release and turn out.

Smoked mackerel pâté with pickled blackberries on seeded toast

Classic flavour combinations done right and simply done: sometimes, it's the simple things in life we crave and this has to be one of them. This is an easy Saturday afternoon brunch to snack on, or it can be dressed up and downsized to impress when made into little canapés for a party or as a starter. Either way, it's comforting, familiar and the perfect match for pickled fruit or vegetables.

Makes 300g (10½oz) pâté, enough for 6–8 toasts

150g (5½oz) skinless smoked mackerel fillets (Home-smoked, page 209)
2 Tbsp unsalted butter, cubed, at room temperature
3–4 Tbsp crème fraîche
1–2 Tbsp fresh horseradish (or to taste), finely grated, or 2 Tbsp horseradish sauce
2 tsp wholegrain or Dijon mustard
zest and juice of ½ lemon
sea salt and freshly ground black pepper, to taste

To serve
sliced seeded bread
rocket (arugula) or baby watercress
Pickled Blackberries (page 40)

In a food processor, blitz together the mackerel, butter, crème fraîche, horseradish, mustard, lemon zest and juice. Taste and season with salt and pepper as you go, adding more crème fraîche if it needs it and pushing the mixture down with a spatula to make sure everything is blended to the same consistency. Remove to a bowl and use immediately or cover and refrigerate before using.

To serve, toast your bread and slather each piece with a healthy spread of pâté. Sprinkle on the rocket or watercress and place a few pickled blackberries on top. Season generously with freshly ground pepper, if needed.

If you don't eat all the pâté in one sitting, it will keep in an airtight container in the fridge for 4–5 days.

Notes
- Try pickled cherries, grapes, gooseberries, blueberries, cucumbers, cornichons, fennel, beetroot (beets) or radishes.
- If you can't get crème fraîche, you can use mascarpone and add 2 teaspoons of olive oil and a squeeze more lemon juice to loosen it up.

Mum's chocolate mousse with sweet pickled raspberries

Mum wouldn't ever have put pickled raspberries with her Christmas chocolate mousse. Instead, we would eat this with fresh strawberries on the side. In New Zealand, it's summertime at Christmas and strawberries are in full season. Now I live in the northern hemisphere, and I see this as a recipe for all-year-round by using pickled fruits instead. I find the pickled element gives this dessert more of an edge.

Makes 4 x 150ml (5fl oz) pots

150ml (⅔ cup) Quick Sweet Pickle Brine, 1:1:1 (page 39), using 60ml (¼ cup) rice or white wine vinegar, 60ml (¼ cup) water and 60g (5 Tbsp) sugar, and spiced with the zest and juice of ½ lemon, ½ cinnamon stick, 1 tsp vanilla extract, 1 star anise and 2 slices of fresh ginger
100g (3½oz) raspberries or other seasonal berries
toasted nuts, to serve (optional)

Mousse
300g (10½oz) milk chocolate (34–37 per cent cocoa solids)
small pinch of salt
200ml (generous ¾ cup) double (heavy) cream, plus (optional) extra to serve
2 large free-range eggs, separated

Make up the brine and pickle your berries 4–12 hours prior to making this recipe and store in the fridge.

Break up the chocolate and melt in a heatproof bowl set over a pan of simmering water until smooth (I sometimes like a few unmelted bits though). Stir through the salt and let cool to room temperature.

In a stand mixer with the whisk attachment or with an electric hand whisk, whip the cream until it is firm (1–2 minutes on a medium-high speed), then transfer to a bowl, if necessary, and chill in the fridge.

Whisk the egg whites in your cleaned stand mixer, or with a hand whisk on a medium-high speed, to stiff peaks (2–3 minutes).

In a small bowl, gently beat the egg yolks and stir through the cooled melted chocolate – it will become stiff. Fold through the egg whites with a large metal spoon in 5–6 soft folds, then gently mix through the chilled whipped cream, trying not to lose too much air as you do so otherwise the mousse becomes runny.

Place 4–5 pickled berries in the bottom of your chosen pots and spoon in a little brine. Divide the mousse equally among the pots, then chill in the fridge for at least 3–4 hours until set.

Serve chilled with some extra whipped cream on top and/or some toasted nuts of your choice, if desired.

Notes
- You don't have to do this in separate pots; try one large pretty bowl to present at the table instead.
- Substitute the raspberries for any pickled fruit you may have to hand: cherries, strawberries, peaches, apricots and pears all work really well.
- If you prefer not to have those sharp pickle notes in your dessert, then use fresh fruit drizzled with a fruit syrup or jam (if you have a sweeter tooth) or compote (if not).
- Or just serve it straight, without fruit additions.

Ferment

Lacto-fermentation

Some "pickles" you might come across are actually the product of fermentation. This process, formally known as lacto-fermentation, is a type of pickling itself.

All fruit, vegetables, grains and dairy products have lactic acid-producing bacteria on them called lactobacilli. In fermentation, these bacteria are encouraged to multiply under a salted brine in a controlled oxygen-free environment, until they produce enough lactic acid to preserve the contents of their jar. This process has been used for thousands of years, long before refrigeration existed, and can be seen in a lot of everyday foods: cheese, vinegar, bread, wine and beer are all processed using natural lacto-bacteria.

Produce

Use fresh, seasonal vegetables that are firm to the touch. Wash them, cutting away any browning or rotting bits. Experiment with different vegetables using the salt-water brine percentages (page 59) for guidance. Different vegetables will take different times to ferment depending on their structure.

Salt

This is the key ingredient in vegetable fermentation, deterring unwanted bacteria while encouraging the good bacteria to get to work. In this chapter, we ferment using a salted-water brine or we extract the moisture by massaging salt into shredded vegetables. It's best to use unprocessed sea salts for their purity. Iodine (table) salts can sometimes taint the process.

Water

Use filtered water so that your ferments get all the nutrients they need. Boiled water often lacks the good minerals needed for fermentation, while tap water can have too much chlorine, killing the probiotic lactobacillus bacteria. If you don't have filtered water, then leave your water in a covered bowl for 24 hours to dechlorinate it.

To make a brine add the salt to your water and stir to dissolve. I suggest dissolving the salt in 100ml (generous ⅓ cup) of boiling water first, letting it cool, then adding it to the remaining measure of filtered water.

Spices

Experiment with a variety. Start with classic combinations, then try new things out. Spices tend to become more extreme in flavour when fermenting, so don't over-spice to begin with! Start mild.

Equipment

- Large, food-safe containers, such as crock pots or jars with lids
- Weights - you don't have to invest in ceramic or glass ones; improvise with what you have in the house to weight vegetables or fruits down
- Muslin (cheesecloth) and elastic bands for covering the jar top, protecting it from dust and fruit flies while fermenting with the lid off
- If you really want to explore fermentation, you can get a pH thermometer or pH strips to test whether your ferments have the correct acid levels for longevity, but these are not essential.

Fermenting brine process

Vegetables must be completely submerged under a salted brine to keep an anaerobic environment, which prevents oxidation and moulding. In some recipes, we use a salt-water brine; in others, you can extract the liquid from the vegetable itself with salt.

Make sure you clean, rinse and dry (or sterilize - page 212) your jars and vessels. Do not use plastics or metals as they could deteriorate.

For liquid extraction, for sauerkraut recipes (pages 60-61), tightly pack handfuls of the cabbage mixture into a large, clean jar with a wide neck, firmly compressing each handful with your fist. Pour over any excess liquid from the bowl and continue to compress with your fist until you have extracted enough brine for all of the vegetables to be generously submerged. Leave enough of a gap at the top of the jar to force in an outer cabbage leaf without it overflowing or weight it down with something that ensures the brine completely covers the ferment.

When using a salt-water brine to ferment, use the salt ratio chart opposite. This technique is used when making Kimchi (page 62). Mix up the salt ratio brine before completely covering and then weighting your ferment.

To keep the vegetables submerged, ceramic or sterilized glass weights can be used or try a plate with a sterilized rock on top, or baking stones in a muslin (cheesecloth) bag. I've even used a bit of parchment or a cabbage leaf pushed and wedged firmly down into the jar. You just need to ensure that the vegetables aren't floating and are under the brine.

Clean down the sides of the jar and cover the top with a piece of muslin secured with an elastic band. Leave in a dark cupboard at room temperature (ideally 18-22°C/64-72°F) for at least 3 days and up to 4 weeks. Taste test it along the way until it's agreeable to your palate.

Fermentation produces gases and sometimes fizz or bubbles. Some vessels may need "burping" to release these gases, if they are sealed too tight or don't have a valve to allow the gases to be released automatically. Instead of a lid, I like to cover mine with muslin squares secured with an elastic band - this enables them to breathe without having to burp the jar. I then seal the jar when it's ready for refrigeration and I can slow down the fermentation process.

Time

Fermentation times vary. The longer you leave them, the more sour and sometimes bubbly the ferments will become. Where you leave them and at what temperature will also affect the readiness. Lactobacilli generally thrive at 18-24°C (64-75°F). At cooler temperatures they'll take longer; higher and they'll be quicker. Check every 2-3 days by removing the weights, scraping off any mould and tasting the vegetable. It's ready when it tastes good to you. This can take anywhere from 4 days to 4 weeks.

Once you're happy with the taste, store in the fridge. This won't stop the bacteria from growing, but slows the process down considerably. They will keep like this for up to 6 months.

Troubleshooting

If you follow the correct process, not a lot can go wrong with lacto-fermentation. It will, however, begin to smell after a few days, when fermentation starts to occur. This can be confusing – it should never smell too foul and unpleasant. Always smell and taste your ferment. It should taste sour and fermented, not mouldy and off – trust your instincts. Mould may grow if anything is exposed directly to oxygen. If the mould is light and pale white, then just scrape it off; if it is black, purple or pink, and big and bumpy, then this indicates that you haven't followed the process correctly. The salt should be acting as a defence against bad bacteria. In this instance, start again.

If you are worried, invest in some pH strips and test that your ferments are under pH 4. There are a lot of websites that have images for reference when things have gone really bad – just google "troubleshooting fermentation".

Salt ratio chart

Below is a general guide to the percentages of salt needed to make a salt-water brine for a given vegetable. For example, if fermenting something with a 2% salt-water brine, you need to mix 1000ml (34fl oz or 4 cups) water with 20g (¾oz or 4 tsp) salt or 500ml (17fl oz or 2 cups) water with 10g (⅓oz or 2 tsp) salt.

Use this to experiment with a variety of different pickles at your leisure – just add spices and time.

Asparagus	5–5.5%	Garlic	3%
Beetroot (beets)	2%	Green beans	2%
Broccoli	2–2.5%	Jalapeños	4.5–5%
Brussels sprouts	2%	Leeks	5%
Cabbage	2–2.5%	Okra	3.5%
Capers, Nasturtium	4.5–5%	Onions	5%
Carrots	2–3%	Peas	2–3%
Cauliflower	2%	Peppers (bell peppers/ capsicums)	4–5%
Celery	1–2%	Potatoes	2%
Chillies	4–5%	Radishes, all types	5%
Courgette (zucchini)	4.5–5%	Tomatoes	2%
Cucumber	4–5%	Turnips	2%
Daikon radish	5%	Mixed vegetables	4.5–5%

White cabbage sauerkraut

Sauerkraut is thought to have originated in China, where shredded cabbage was soured in a rice wine, but is now more widely associated with eastern European cuisines, where it is widely eaten and served with many things from sausages to soups. The Germans gave it the moniker "sauerkraut", which translates to "sour cabbage". The following recipe is a classic white cabbage sauerkraut. As you become more confident with the process, you can create your own flavour combinations and introduce new vegetables using this recipe as a base.

Makes about 600g (1lb 5oz)

750g (1lb 10oz) white cabbage, sliced into very thin ribbons about 3–5mm (⅛–¼in) wide (use a mandoline, if you have one, or a very sharp knife, or carefully use a peeler to shave off strips along the grain). Leave 1 large outer cabbage leaf unsliced for later if you don't have weights.
3 tsp sea salt
½ apple, peeled and grated
1 tsp caraway seeds
1 tsp juniper berries or black peppercorns

Weigh the shredded cabbage in a large bowl. For every 500g (1lb 2oz), mix through 2 teaspoons of sea salt. With clean hands or wearing latex gloves, massage the salt into the cabbage with some force for 5 minutes, until it starts to release moisture and is glossy in appearance. Cover and set aside for 40–60 minutes at room temperature.

Add the grated apple to the cabbage along with the caraway seeds and juniper berries/peppercorns and mix through with your hands.

Using a clean 1 litre (34fl oz) jar with a wide neck, follow the packing method and timings on page 58.

Once fermented, remove the cabbage leaf or weight, clean the sides of the jar of any mould and keep sealed in the fridge. Eat within 6 weeks.

Notes
- Add different spices, such as turmeric, chilli flakes, lemon or orange slices, fennel seeds, coriander or cumin seeds.
- Try half the weight of sliced cabbage mixed with half of grated mooli (daikon radish) or carrot. Play around with different cabbages (Savoy, Brussels sprouts) using the Salt Ratio Chart to guide you (page 59).

Red cabbage and beetroot sauerkraut

Sauerkraut is really easy to make. Once you start making it, you'll find you never actually have to buy it again – you can have one jar fermenting and another in the fridge, rotating jars so you will never run out. It is often healthier for you, too. When you make it yourself, you are getting all the healthy probiotics that some commercially made ones won't have after the pasteurization process. If you are buying it, make sure you pick one that is handmade, stored in the fridge and possibly bubbling over with a stained label – that way you know the bacteria are alive and active.

Makes about 600g (1lb 5oz)

450g (1lb) red (or white) cabbage, sliced into very thin ribbons about 3–5mm (⅛–¼in) wide (use a mandoline, if you have one, or a very sharp knife, or carefully use a peeler to shave off strips along the grain). Leave 1 large outer cabbage leaf unsliced for later if you don't have weights.
300g (10½oz) raw beetroot (beets), peeled and grated
3 tsp sea salt
4cm (1½in) piece of horseradish or root ginger (optional), peeled and finely grated
1 tsp caraway seeds

Place the cabbage along with the grated beetroot into a large bowl and weigh the prepped vegetables. For every 500g (1lb 2oz) add 2 teaspoons of sea salt. With clean hands or wearing latex gloves, massage the salt into the vegetables with some force for 5 minutes, until they start to release moisture and are glossy in appearance. Cover and set aside for 40–60 minutes at room temperature.

Add the horseradish or ginger along with the caraway seeds and use your hands to mix through.

Using a clean 1 litre (34fl oz) jar with a wide neck, follow the packing method and timings on page 58.

Once fermented, remove the cabbage leaf or weight, clean the sides of the jar of any mould and keep sealed in the fridge. Eat within 6 weeks.

Notes
- Play with different spices, such as chilli flakes, juniper berries, turmeric or fennel seeds.
- Add a bit of grated apple to add sour notes to the flavour; for a sweeter palate, try a small handful of raisins.

Kimchi

Kimchi is much like sauerkraut, only using a salt-water brine rather than an extracted brine, and the ingredients and spices are influenced by a different part of the world: Korea. Kimchi is not only a staple food in Korea, it is a way of life and a large part of the everyday culture, being individual not only to different regions but to each family. There are a lot of different kimchi recipes to experiment with. This recipe is a starter recipe if you are new to fermentation, but it is worth exploring the depths of this fantastic dish and discovering its importance to the Korean community. I recommend reading the book *Kimchi: Essential recipes of the Korean Kitchen* by Byung-Hi Lim and Byung-Soon Lim to discover more.

Lacto-ferments tend to work best with a 2–5% brine solution (some vegetables needing stronger brine than others). Traditionally, kimchi brines are around 15%, but they tend to taste very salty. So, for this recipe, I like to use a 4% brine – not too salty, but enough to aid the fermentation process.

Makes about 750g (1lb 10oz)

1 litre (4 cups) filtered water
40g (8 tsp) sea salt
750g (1lb 10oz) Napa cabbage/
   Chinese lettuce
250g (9oz) mooli/daikon radish
   (about 1 medium)
500g (1lb 2oz) carrots (about 3
   large)
1 banana shallot or 2 round shallots,
   finely diced

Spice paste
1 small onion (90–100g/3–3½oz),
   chopped
2–3 garlic cloves (15–18g/½oz),
   peeled
5cm (2in) piece of fresh ginger
   (40–50g/1½–2oz), peeled
3 Tbsp gochugaru powder/paste
   (Korean dried red chilli powder/
   paste) or cayenne pepper

Make up your 4% salt-water brine (pages 56 and 59).

Cut the Napa into chunky slices about 5–6cm (2in) wide for the thinner top part and thinner slices about 1–2cm (½–¾in) wide for the denser base part. It is up to you how you chop, but keep in mind how you want to present/eat it as a finished ferment. Ribbon the mooli and carrots into long, thin, wide strips using a potato peeler, turning the vegetables as you work to get the widest strips you can. Alternatively, you can use a mandoline to create ribbons or cut into very thin discs.

In a large container, mix the cabbage, mooli and carrots with your hands. Pour over the brine so that it completely covers the vegetables (make up more brine if you need to). Weight the vegetables down under the salt brine with a plate or weights, cover and leave at room temperature for up to 8 hours or overnight.

Drain off the brine, reserving 600ml (2½ cups). Mix through the diced shallot into the strained vegetables.

To make the spice paste, add 100ml (generous ⅓ cup) of the reserved brine to a food processor along with the chopped onion, garlic, ginger and gochugaru, and blend until completely smooth.

With gloved hands, and using a clean 1 litre (34fl oz) jar with a wide neck, follow the packing method and timings on page 59.

Once fermented, remove the weight, clean the sides of the jar of any mould and keep sealed in the fridge. Eat within 6 weeks.

Note
- This naturally fermented kimchi might be more sour than store-bought
  ones, which often aren't vegan and may contain stabilizers. Add 1 tablespoon
  of fish sauce or miso to your spice paste to make a sweeter version if that's to
  your taste.

Potato and sauerkraut knishes with pickled cabbage and soured cream

I made my first knish when I was asked to develop a menu for a supper club in London called Kino Vino, where the concept was that the host, Alissa Timoshkina, picked a foreign film and asked cooks to create a meal influenced by it. My film was *Crossing Delancey*, a 1980s film about a Jewish girl who eventually falls for a pickle vendor in New York. During my research, I discovered these delightful potato and sauerkraut knishes, a Jewish snack that I like to pair with pickled cabbage and soured cream and have for lunch.

Makes 8

Pastry
100g (scant ½ cup) unsalted butter
280g (generous 2 cups) plain
    (all-purpose) flour, plus extra
    for dusting
1 tsp baking powder
½ tsp sea salt
2 free-range eggs, lightly beaten
1 tsp white wine vinegar
3 Tbsp water

Quick Pickled Red Cabbage
200g (7oz) red cabbage, very finely
    shredded
175ml (¾ cup) Quick Pickle Brine,
    3:2:1 (page 17) using white
    wine vinegar and spiced with
    ½ tsp sea salt, ¼ tsp black
    peppercorns, ¼ tsp chilli (red
    pepper) flakes, ½ tsp mustard
    seeds, 1 bay leaf and the juice
    of ½ lime

Filling
450g (1lb) potatoes, roughly
    chopped
1 Tbsp light olive oil, rapeseed or
    vegetable oil
1 banana shallot or small onion, very
    finely diced
1–2 garlic cloves, finely chopped
150g (5½oz) White Cabbage
    Sauerkraut (page 60), strained
150g (generous 1½ cups) cream
    cheese
80ml (⅓ cup) water
2 tsp za'atar (or a mix of dried thyme
    with sesame seeds)
1 egg, beaten
2 tsp sesame or poppy seeds
sea salt and freshly ground black
    pepper, to taste

Prepare the pastry at least 8 hours in advance. Also, make up the quick pickled red cabbage at least 3–4 hours before you plan to serve.

To make the pastry, first melt the butter and set aside to cool. In a stand mixer fitted with the paddle attachment or in a large bowl, sift the dry ingredients and mix together. In a separate bowl, mix the cooled butter with the beaten eggs, vinegar and water, then slowly pour into the dry ingredients, mixing on a medium speed until combined.

Change to the hook attachment on the mixer and knead for 3–5 minutes until the pastry is soft and malleable, or knead by hand in the bowl for 5–7 minutes. When ready, place the dough into a rectangular Tupperware container (about 17 x 12 x 6cm/7 x 5 x 2½in), gently push the dough into the corners, seal and refrigerate for 8–24 hours.

To make the filling, boil the potatoes in a large covered saucepan of salted water for 10–12 minutes, or until they are soft enough to mash.

Meanwhile, heat the oil in a large frying pan over a medium heat, add the shallot or onion, season with salt and pepper and sauté for 4–5 minutes until soft and translucent. Add the garlic and sauerkraut and cook for another 4–5 minutes until some of the moisture has cooked out of the sauerkraut.

Drain the potatoes, add the cream cheese and water and mash until reasonably smooth but still with a few lumps. Stir through the sauerkraut mixture along with the za'atar.

(continues)

Potato and sauerkraut knishes *continued*

To serve
2–3 Tbsp soured cream or crème fraîche

Remove the pastry from the fridge and cut it in half. Return one half to the fridge while you work. On a lightly floured work surface, roll out the dough to as neat a rectangle as possible, 40 x 18cm (16 x 7in). Keeping a long side facing you, gently score the pastry into sections. Start by dividing it in half length-ways, then divide the section nearest to you into four crossways; each section will be 10cm (4in) wide.

Divide the filling into 8 portions (roughly 70g/2½oz each), leaving extra aside to top up each knish. Place a portion of filling into the middle of each marked section, then gently lift the top half of the pastry dough up and over the filling to cover. Fold the long edge of the pastry over by about 1cm (½in) to seal the join. Gently make indentations in the pastry with the side of your hand between the mounds of filling, then use a sharp knife to cut along the indentations to separate them into four segments. Seal each segment by twisting the dough on one side of these cut ends, then sit it upright on this sealed twist. Open up the top end and spoon in an extra heaped teaspoon of filling before making a decorative twist to seal completely. Place on a large parchment-lined baking sheet.

Repeat until you have made 8 knishes using the remaining pastry and chill in the fridge for 30 minutes.

Meanwhile, preheat the oven to 200°C (180°C fan/400°F/gas mark 6).

Brush the knishes with egg wash and sprinkle over the sesame or poppy seeds. Bake in the middle of the oven for 45 minutes until golden, turning the baking sheet halfway through so they cook evenly.

Best eaten hot from the oven and served with soured cream or crème fraîche and quick pickled cabbage.

Notes
- These keep well in an airtight container in the fridge for 2–3 days. To serve, warm through in a low oven for 20–30 minutes.
- Alternatively, eat cold as a snack with some chutney, such as the Green Tomato Chutney (page 84) or Gooseberry Chutney (page 84).

Polish mushroom and sauerkraut pierogis with burnt butter and soured cream

Traditionally, sauerkraut pierogis are made for Christmas Eve, when the Polish celebrate Christmas. They are made to feed many people, so recipes often make up hundreds at a time, but they do freeze well. I love the idea that the family gather together and spend the day at the table making them, working and chatting and drinking wine (at least, this was my experience with my very good friend Karolina who first taught me to make these little pockets of delight). My husband's grandmother was Polish, so I hope to keep some of her traditions alive now that she is no longer with us. My version has been scaled down to a more manageable size.

Makes 30 (serves 4–5)

Dough
260g (2 cups) plain (all-purpose) flour, plus extra for dusting
pinch of sea salt
1 free-range egg
90ml (⅓ cup) warm water, more if needed

Filling
25g (1oz) dried mushrooms (oyster or porcini)
250ml (1 cup) boiling water
2 Tbsp light olive, rapeseed (canola) or vegetable oil, plus extra for drizzling
1 banana shallot or small onion (about 100g/3½oz), very finely diced
100g (3½oz) button or chestnut (cremini) mushrooms, cleaned and very finely diced
170g (6oz) White Cabbage Sauerkraut (page 60)
sea salt and freshly ground black pepper

To serve
100g (scant ½ cup) unsalted butter
200g (scant 1 cup) soured cream or crème fraîche

At least 1 hour before you begin to make the dough, place the dried mushrooms in a bowl, cover with the boiling water and leave to soak.

Sift together the flour and salt in a large bowl. In a separate bowl, whisk the egg with the warm water. Use a fork to mix the egg/water through the flour until it starts to just come together, then use your hands to bring it together, adding more water only if needed – the dough shouldn't be too tacky, nor too dry.

Turn out the dough onto a lightly floured work surface and knead for 5–8 minutes until smooth and glossier in appearance. Wrap the dough in a slightly damp dish towel and let rest in a cool place for 30 minutes, without letting it dry out too much.

Meanwhile, heat the oil in a large frying pan, add the shallot or onion, season generously with salt and pepper and sauté for 4–5 minutes, until glossy and translucent. Add the fresh mushrooms and sauté for 4–5 minutes. Drain the dried mushrooms (reserving the soaking water) and roughly chop. Add to the pan along with 100ml (generous ⅓ cup) of the soaking water and cook for 4–5 minutes until the liquid has evaporated and the mixture starts to get slightly sticky on the bottom. Strain the sauerkraut by giving it a good squeeze and add to the pan to cook off any excess moisture.

Cut the dough in half, keeping one half covered by the dish towel. On a lightly floured work surface, roll out the dough to 2mm (⅛in) thick, rotating and flipping it between rolls. With a 9cm (3½in) cookie

(continues)

Mushroom and sauerkraut pierogis *continued*

cutter or the rim of a glass, cut out as many circles as you can. Reserve the scraps and place with the dough under the dish towel.

Place a heaped teaspoon of the filling in the middle of each circle of dough, then fold and stretch the dough up over the filling, gently pushing the filling in so it doesn't spill out. Firmly pinch the edges of the dough together, starting from the middle, to seal tightly. Place on a clean dry cloth (not touching each other) and cover while you repeat rolling, filling and sealing until you have run out of either dough or filling.

Bring a very large saucepan of water to a vigorous boil with a pinch of salt and drop in the pierogis, one by one, cooking them in batches of 5 or 6 at a time. Cook for 3 minutes or until they start to float to the surface. Fish out with a slotted spoon and add to a bowl with a drizzle of oil, so they don't stick together.

Heat the butter in a small frying pan until it starts to sizzle and smell nutty, and turns brown.

You can eat your pierogis just boiled with a drizzle of the burnt butter, or fry them in the brown butter pan for 1 minute on each side until golden. Serve with the butter on the side for extra drizzling and a dollop of soured cream.

Notes
- These are *kiszona kapusta* (sauerkraut) pierogis, but there are other delicious fillings using this dough to discover, such as the much celebrated *ruskie twarog* (potato and soft cheese).
- Try sweet fillings of chopped fruits macerated in your homemade jams. Use the same boiling technique then fry in butter. Serve sweet versions with vanilla ice cream or sweetened yoghurt.

Celeriac and apple soup, beetroot sauerkraut and buckwheat crackers

Add a dollop of any type of sauerkraut you have in the fridge to a warming winter soup. The sharp sourness is great for cutting through creamier textures, and adding a topping like pumpkin seeds creates a bit of crunch. Try different soup/sauerkraut combinations to make it a proper fridge forage.

Serves 4–6

2 tsp butter
1 Tbsp olive oil
1 large onion, diced
1 celery stalk, diced
½ tsp chilli (red pepper) flakes (optional)
1 sprig of fresh thyme or lemon thyme
1 litre (4 cups) vegetable stock
650–700g (1lb 7oz–1lb 9oz) celeriac (celery root), peeled and diced
1 sharp-tasting apple, peeled, cored and diced
sea salt and freshly ground black pepper

To serve
handful of pumpkin seeds
1–2 Tbsp Red Cabbage and Beetroot Sauerkraut (page 61)
1–2 Buckwheat and Pumpkin-Seed Crackers (page 201)

Prep all your vegetables before you start: washing, peeling and chopping.

In a large heavy-based pan, melt the butter with the oil over a medium heat. Add the onion, season liberally, and cook for about 4 minutes, stirring, until it starts to sizzle. Add the celery, chilli flakes and thyme and gently sauté for 10–15 minutes until the onion and celery are soft, glossy and translucent, gently caramelized yet not too browned.

Meanwhile, in another saucepan, warm the stock over a medium–low heat. Add a small ladleful to the onion pan and cook it off for 1 minute or so until dry. Add the celeriac and apple to the onion pan and cook, stirring for 4–5 minutes, adding ladlefuls of warm stock as you go. Pour in the remaining stock, bring to a simmer and cook on a medium–low heat for 25–30 minutes or until the celeriac is soft.

Toast the pumpkin seeds in a small pan over a medium heat with a healthy pinch of sea salt. Take them off the heat when they start cracking and popping and are slightly browned. Set aside for garnish.

Remove the soup from the heat and let cool slightly, then blend in a food processor or with a hand-held stick blender until smooth.

When ready to serve, warm through and add a dollop of sauerkraut, a sprinkle of pumpkin seeds and serve with a side of buckwheat crackers.

Notes
- Mix it up with alternatives. Try: pumpkin soup, red cabbage sauerkraut and toasted pumpkin seeds; beetroot (beet) soup, white cabbage sauerkraut and toasted hazelnuts; cream of mushroom soup, beetroot sauerkraut and toasted buckwheat.
- It's nice to add a dollop of soured cream or crème fraîche as well.

Red cabbage and beetroot sauerkraut slaw with baked chickpeas

This is a great way to use up a lot of sauerkraut sitting in your condiment ghost-town in your fridge. It's simple, delicious and a great addition to any barbecue or a selection of salads. Match this slaw with the Buttermilk Fried Chicken from the tacos recipe (page 34) or as a side to a Pickled Pea Frittata (page 24). Or simply eat it by itself as the chickpeas add that plant-based protein you need for a balanced meal. You can also use the brine drained from canned chickpeas (called aquafaba) in other recipes – see notes below.

Serves 4–6

200g (1½ cups) canned chickpeas (garbanzo beans), drained, rinsed and dried
2 Tbsp olive oil
½ tsp caraway seeds, gently crushed
1 tsp ground cumin
sea salt and freshly ground black pepper

Slaw

150g (5½oz) Red Cabbage and Beetroot Sauerkraut (page 61)
150g (5½oz) white cabbage, very finely shredded
1 small carrot, grated (optional)
100g (scant ½ cup) mayonnaise (Homemade, page 203)
½ apple, peeled and grated
1 small orange, cut into 1cm (½in) cubes
1 tsp yellow or brown mustard seeds
handful of fresh coriander (cilantro) or flat-leaf parsley, roughly chopped, plus extra to serve
freshly ground black pepper

Preheat the oven to 200°C (180°C fan/400°F/gas mark 6).

Combine the chickpeas with the olive oil in a bowl, season generously with salt and pepper, then add the caraway and cumin. Mix until the chickpeas are well coated, then evenly spread them in a single layer over a baking sheet. Bake in the middle of the oven for 15–20 minutes, tossing every 5 minutes, until crisp and golden. Remove from the oven and leave to cool to room temperature.

Measure out the sauerkraut and squeeze out any excess brine. In a large bowl, mix the sauerkraut with the raw shredded white cabbage and grated carrot, if using, then stir through the mayonnaise. Season generously with pepper, then mix through the apple, orange pieces, mustard seeds and fresh herbs until well combined.

Serve the slaw in a large bowl or dish with the baked chickpeas and more herbs sprinkled on top as your main meal or a side salad. It is great served for a quick lunch with sides of Homemade Flatbreads (page 193) and Labneh (page 204). It is best eaten on the same day, but can be stored in an airtight container in the fridge for 2–3 days.

Notes
- Alternatively, you can use White Cabbage Sauerkraut (page 60) with shredded raw red cabbage.
- Try ½ diced grapefruit instead of the orange or omit the citrus flesh altogether and add a healthy squeeze of lime or lemon juice.
- Make sure to save the aquafaba drained off the chickpeas. This is a great substitute for egg whites in many recipes, such as vegan meringue (page 166), vegan aïoli (page 203) or in cocktails, such as whisky or amaretto sours. Just substitute 1 egg white for 3 tablespoons of aquafaba.

Breakfast kimchi eggs

"Kimchi for breakfast?" you might say. Yep, once you've had it, you won't be able to go back to your ordinary eggy breakfast. Try kimchi in eggs two ways: scrambled or as an omelette.

Scramble

Serves 2

1 Tbsp cooking oil
150–200g (5½–7oz) Kimchi (page 62), roughly chopped
4 free-range eggs, lightly beaten
1 Tbsp crème fraîche (optional)

To serve
sourdough toast, buttered
handful of flat-leaf parsley, roughly chopped (optional)
sea salt and freshly ground black pepper

Heat the oil in a medium frying pan or skillet over a medium-high heat. When hot, add the kimchi and cook for 2–3 minutes, stirring. Pour in the beaten eggs and cook untouched for 20–30 seconds before pushing them around the pan to scramble and mix in with the kimchi. Cook for a further 1–2 minutes, or longer if you like your eggs well done.

Stir through the crème fraîche and serve on buttered sourdough toast, seasoned with salt and pepper and sprinkled with parsley, if wished.

Omelette

Makes 1

2 large free-range eggs
1 tsp mirin or ½ tsp sugar
2 tsp kimchi brine from the jar
1 Tbsp cooking oil or butter
50g (2oz) Kimchi (page 62), finely chopped
green part of 1 spring onion (scallion), finely chopped
40–50g (1½–2oz) strong mature Cheddar or Gruyère cheese, grated
sea salt and freshly ground black pepper

To serve (optional)
hot sauce
small handful of flat-leaf parsley, roughly chopped

In a bowl, gently whisk the eggs with the mirin and kimchi brine.

Heat half of the oil or butter in a medium frying pan or skillet over a medium-high heat. When hot, add the kimchi and cook for 1–2 minutes, stirring, until you have fried off some of the moisture. Remove and set aside.

Heat the remaining oil or butter in the same pan. When hot, add the spring onion and cook for about 1–2 minutes, then pour in the egg mixture. Season with salt and pepper and cook for 1–2 minutes or until the egg is not-quite set. Sprinkle over the grated cheese and cooked kimchi, then fold the omelette in half and cook for a final 1–2 minutes until the cheese has melted.

Serve with a drizzle of hot sauce, if you are daring, and chopped flat-leaf parsley or with sourdough toast and crème fraîche as above.

Kimchi fried rice with a fried egg

I grew up with Asian-inspired meals, as my mum was quite an adventurous cook for the time, and New Zealand has a large cosmopolitan culture with a lot of influences from the Pacific Rim. Therefore, egg fried rice has always been a staple of mine. It's an easy, go-to meal when I haven't got a lot of time and that I can make with little energy or thought. Adding kimchi (especially if it's homemade) makes it extra-special and comforting.

Serves 2–3

Fried rice
250g (generous 2 cups) pre-cooked/steamed rice (see method)
1–2 Tbsp vegetable, sunflower or rapeseed (canola) oil, plus extra if needed
1 banana shallot, diced
100g (¾ cup) frozen or fresh peas
200g (7oz) Kimchi (page 62), cut into 2cm (¾in) pieces
1 large egg
1 Tbsp sesame oil
1 Tbsp kimchi brine from the jar or soy sauce
bunch of coriander (cilantro), roughly chopped
sea salt and freshly ground black pepper, to taste

Fried eggs (optional)
1 Tbsp vegetable, sunflower or rapeseed (canola) oil or butter
2–3 large eggs

To serve (optional)
1 spring onion (scallion), sliced
Sriracha or other hot sauce

Pre-cook your rice at least 1 hour and up to 24 hours beforehand. This is a great recipe if you have made too much rice the night before, as you want the rice to be drier for frying. For food safety, if you are making it well in advance, cool and refrigerate the rice as soon as possible after cooking, then bring to room temperature before making this dish.

For the fried rice, heat the vegetable oil in a medium frying pan or preferably a wok over a medium heat. Gently stir-fry the shallot for 4–6 minutes until caramelized – take care not to let it burn. Add the peas and kimchi, increase the heat, and cook for 1–2 minutes. Reduce the heat slightly and add the rice. Stir-fry for 4–5 minutes, adding a little more oil if it's looking a bit dry.

Gently whisk the egg with the sesame oil and kimchi brine. Make a well in the middle of the rice and pour in the egg mix. Let it cook undisturbed for 15–20 seconds, then stir it through to thoroughly coat the rice. Taste and season with salt, then stir through the coriander. Reduce the heat to low while you fry your eggs.

For the fried eggs, heat the oil or butter in a non-stick frying pan over a medium–high heat. Crack in the eggs and as soon as you hear them start to sizzle cover with a lid. Fry for 30 seconds, then turn off the heat and leave covered for a further 30 seconds (so they steam). Depending on how runny you like your egg, you can cook them for longer, but the runnier the better for breaking over the kimchi rice.

Serve an egg on top of each serving of kimchi rice, sprinkled with spring onion and a zig-zag squeeze of Sriracha or other hot sauce.

Note
- If you don't have any kimchi, this dish is equally as tasty without. For that bit
  of zing you could add a mixed tablespoon of cayenne pepper and garlic salt
  or gochugaru (Korean dried red chilli powder) to mimic the flavour.

Chutneys, relishes and sauces

The following chapter is mostly chutneys. Although chutney originates in India (where it is a much fresher, more immediate condiment) these are more Anglicized versions, with the added preservation elements of sugar and vinegar.

After pickling, chutneys and sauces are the next easiest thing to create when preserving. The idea is to boil a combination of fruit and vegetables with sugar, vinegar and spices until they become thick and sticky. They are then jarred while hot, which creates a heat vacuum seal, enabling longevity. The sugar and vinegar also contribute to a longer, preserved, life.

This preserving technique is a great way of using up a seasonal glut, but it is also a good way to use up the older, less fresh and even browning fruit or vegetables that you might otherwise discard, so creating less food waste. The ingredients don't have to be fresh, as we are not relying on pectin, which we need for making jam; rather, we are boiling and reducing to make a thickened and sticky consistency.

You can make quick chutneys, to be eaten within a week, but the acidity in vinegar tends to be very sharp at the beginning and they tend to need a lot more sugar for a balanced flavour. When we jar and store a chutney for a few weeks, these acidic beginnings will mellow and infuse with the spices in the jar, improving the flavour over time (unless you are making an authentic Indian one, where there's very little cooking involved at all and it's a very different process).

Produce

Use fresh or aging fruit and vegetables. Always wash and prep your produce. Peel where necessary and make sure you cut your fruit and vegetables into 5mm–1cm (¼–½in) cubes or as close as possible (unless you are making a sauce that you are going to blend into a purée later). This may sound insignificant, but you will get the best results in your reduction this way, as the matter has a smaller circumference to break down and cook. It also makes for a pleasant size for eating, especially if you like to add chutney to a piece of cheese. I would also emphasize cutting things as you wish to present them on your plate.

Produce for chutneys and sauces normally includes an onion element: use red, white, pink or shallots. Then, there is usually a fruit and/ or a vegetable element. These can vary according to what you have available. The best thing to do if you find yourself with produce that's starting to wane is to whip up a quick chutney.

Vinegars

These are the base liquid for the reduction so the vegetables can start to break down and give you the sweet/sour notes that a chutney provides. Use them all: all different flavours, cider, red and white wine, malt, distilled malt, rice wine, balsamic, sherry. There is no need to use very expensive ones as all the flavours meld into each other, and although some of the vinegar flavours shine through, they won't be the stand-out flavour of the dish. Unlike in a pickle, we are not reliant on an acidity level to create stability; in a chutney, we are using the sugar with the vinegar and heat sterilization to aid longevity.

Sugars

Sugars are needed to balance the sharpness of the vinegar. As it's a reduction game, use darker, richer sugars that are full of flavour: dark and light brown sugars, muscovado or golden granulated. The caramelized flavours of these sugars work best.

Salt

This is purely used as a flavour enhancer. I tend to add it close to the end of cooking, stirring it through 10 minutes before jarring, to bind the big flavours together.

Spices (and co)

Experiment with your flavour profiles. Build a big spice collection and use them in abundance:
Dried or ground: coriander, fennel, cumin, cloves, cinnamon, peppercorns (black, pink and white), mace, saffron, cardamom (green and black), mustard (yellow and brown), turmeric, juniper berries, bay leaves, chillies (chilli powders/flakes), mint, basil, sage, thyme, rosemary, lemon thyme, lemon verbena, star anise, nutmeg
Fresh: coriander (cilantro), ginger, garlic, chillies, citrus fruit (zest/rind/juice), mint, basil, rosemary, lemon thyme, lemon verbena, sage

There are a couple of ways of adding flavourings. If they are whole spices or pieces that you don't want to bite into (such as whole peppercorns, whole chillies, cinnamon stick, cardamom pods, lemon rind), tie them up neatly into a muslin/spice bag. Simply cut an 18cm (7in) square of muslin (cheesecloth), place the spices in the middle, bring up the corners and twist it tightly around the contents. Tie and securely tuck in all the ends, like a top knot, tightly so it won't release while cooking. If using flavourings that are ground or acceptable to bite into, then just add them directly to the pan with the chopped fruit, vegetables, sugar and vinegar.

Equipment

- Jars and lids that you can sterilize – used jars and lids are suitable, providing they are in good condition, don't have chips or cracks and the lid seals are intact. Make sure when buying new jars and lids to buy good-quality ones that can withstand high heat.
- A large, wide, heavy-based, low-sided pan (avoid aluminium or copper as the vinegars will react) is essential for reduction as it conducts heat more evenly with less height for the steam to run back in.
- A long-handled wooden spoon
- A wide-mouthed funnel
- A heat-safe measuring jug (cup)
- A ladle

Chutney process

The beauty of chutney is that you just add everything to the pan, bring it to the boil and cook for 20-90 minutes to render it down to a sticky consistency. You want to cook it at high heat to render down - this does mean it takes a while and can threaten to stick on the bottom and burn, so watch it and stir consistently throughout cooking.

Always start by sterilizing your jars and lids (page 212) and use hot, straight from the oven.

Some chutneys are sloppier than others. To test whether it is ready to jar, run a wooden spoon across the bottom of the pan: if there is a clear path for at least 5 seconds it should be ready. Some pour into the jars easily, but for the chunkier ones you may need to use a teaspoon to push it down into the jar. Try to remove as many of the trapped air pockets as you can and top up where possible.

Fill the jars as quickly as you can to retain the heat. Use a ladle and wide-mouthed funnel, and fill to 2-3mm (⅛in) from the top of the rim. Clean the rim with a clean damp cloth and seal quickly with sterilized hot lids. You don't want to lose too much heat from the chutney and the jar so that bacteria cannot survive the high temperatures of 100°C (212°F) and over.

Some preservers use a canning bath or heat process after sealing, where the jars are brought to a gentle boil in a bath of water covering them entirely for 10-15 minutes. This can add to the longevity of your preserves and ensure a secure seal, but it can also overcook the chutney. I never do this - if you seal quickly without losing temperature this should be safe enough.

Once cooled, label and date. Chutneys should be kept sealed in a cool, dark place and can keep like this for 12-24 months because of the high sugar and vinegar content. They will be ready to eat in 3-4 weeks but, once opened, they must be stored in the fridge and eaten within 4-6 months.

Troubleshooting

Not a lot can go wrong with chutney because of the long times they are cooked for. Different vegetables may render down at different times. My timings are merely a guide and can vary with the equipment, heat source, how you have cut your vegetables and how much water content they have. These are all elements that will determine how quickly an ingredient reaches its thicker, stickier self. Take your time, it's ready when it's ready, and use your senses.

Keep a keener eye on chutneys towards the end of cooking as this is when they will be inclined to burn if not stirred. I always cook mine on a high heat, and they do start to spit (what I call the teenage phase). When the chutney starts to congeal, it may stick and burn on the bottom of the pan, due to the bubbles finding it harder to release through the thick contents. This creates hot air pockets on the bottom of the pan, encouraging it to burn. Watch more carefully at this point and stir to release those hot air pockets.

Any browned surfaces, once the jar has been opened, means that the seal hasn't worked properly. If you are not using new lids each time, try a perfectly cut round of baking parchment to cover the surface of the chutney before sealing; this acts as an extra layer to protect it from the bacteria in the air. Always fill everything, chutney and jars, at the same temperature, just over 100°C (212°F), to kill off any bacteria, and so that the jars don't crack from differing temperatures.

Green tomato chutney

Makes 5–6 x 250ml (8½fl oz) jars

1kg (2lb 4oz) green unripe tomatoes,
cut into 7mm–1cm (⅜–½in) cubes
350g (12oz) onions, cut into
7mm–1cm (⅜–½in) cubes
350g (12oz) apples, peeled, cored
and cut into 7mm–1cm (⅜–½in)
cubes
300g (1½ cups) light brown, dark
brown or muscovado sugar
550ml (2⅓ cups) cider vinegar
2 tsp mustard seeds, lightly crushed
100g (¾ cup) raisins, optional
1 tsp sea salt

Spice bag

1 tsp black peppercorns
1 lime, washed and chopped into
8–10 pieces
2 bird's-eye chillies, roughly chopped
20g (¾oz) fresh root ginger, roughly
chopped

Sterilize your jars and lids (page 212) and make up
your spice bag (page 81).

Place everything but the raisins and salt into a large,
wide, low-sided, heavy-based, non-reactive pan and
bring to the boil over a medium-high heat. See page
82 for the process of cooking and jarring, reducing
for 30–50 minutes while adding the raisins and salt
20 minutes in.

Note
- If using ripe red tomatoes, cook for longer as they will
have a higher liquid content. If they are particularly
juicy, salt them overnight and drain off the excess
liquid to decrease cooking time.

Gooseberry chutney

Makes 3–4 x 250ml (8½fl oz) jars

1kg (2lb 4oz) green or red
gooseberries, washed, topped
and tailed
300–350g (10½–12oz) banana
shallots or white onion, finely
diced
400g (2 cups) light brown or
muscovado sugar
300ml (1¼ cups) cider vinegar
zest and juice of 2 lemons
1 tsp nigella seeds (optional)
1 tsp sea salt

Spice bag

30g (1oz) fresh root ginger, roughly
chopped
4 cardamom pods
1 tsp crushed chilli
1 tsp black peppercorns

Sterilize your jars and lids (page 212) and make up
your spice bag (page 81).

Place everything but the nigella seeds and salt into
a large, wide, low-sided, heavy-based, non-reactive
pan and bring to the boil over a medium-high heat.
See page 82 for the process of cooking and jarring,
reducing for 30–50 minutes while adding the nigella
seeds and salt 20 minutes in.

Note
- Gooseberries freeze really well, but make sure you
wash, dry, top and tail them before you freeze. Always
defrost them before making this recipe, drain and
increase the cooking time, as they will have retained
a lot of liquid.

Cranberry sauce
(not just for Christmas)

Cranberries and cranberry sauce seem to me to be the "puppies of Christmas". It's important that, once Christmas is over, they don't get forgotten about. As they have an association with Christmas, people don't want anything to do with them afterwards, which is definitely type-casting. I'd like you to consider an all-year-round love of cranberries so in this chapter I offer up other recipes to use them in for the everyday. Homemade cranberry sauce is the best - it's quick and easy and so much better than buying it. I highly recommend making this as you'll never turn back to the overly sweet versions you can get in the shops.

Makes 4–5 x 230ml (8fl oz) jars

500g (5½ cups) cranberries, fresh or frozen, rinsed where necessary
200ml (generous ¾ cup) water (150ml/⅔ cup if using frozen berries)
200g (1 cup) caster (superfine) sugar
½ tsp ground cinnamon
¼ tsp ground ginger

Optional additions
orange zest
port/orange juice/Cointreau/ Campari (if adding liquids, omit 50ml/3½ Tbsp of the original water quantity and add 100ml/ generous ⅓ cup of any of these)

Sterilize your jars and lids (page 212).

Place the cranberries and water into a large, wide, low-sided, heavy-based, non-reactive pan and bring to the boil over a medium–high heat. Cook for 6–8 minutes until they start to crackle, then add the sugar and spices. Gently mash and cook for a further 8–10 minutes over a medium heat, adding your zest, alcohol or juice and stirring occasionally until it thickens.

Once thick and sticky, ladle into sterilized jars according to the chutney jarring and storage process (page 82).

Notes
- Always defrost first if using frozen berries and increase the cooking time.
- There are lots of ways to use up your cranberry sauce so it's not just for Christmas. It matches perfectly with the soft, oozy-type cheeses; for ideas, see pages 98 and 101.

Blackberry and apple chutney

Blackberries tend to hang around until the first frost in the northern hemisphere so you can get them right up until November, making it the perfect time to get a stock of chutneys made for Christmas. I find blackberry chutney the most indulgent of them all, so it fits well into the gluttony and decadence of Christmas. It's best served with rich meats, such as game birds like pheasant, partridge, duck or goose, but is equally good with the after-dinner board of strong, stinky cheeses, fresh fruit and port.

Makes 4–6 x 230ml (8fl oz) jars

600g (1lb 5oz) blackberries, rinsed and patted dry, whole or halved
500ml (2 cups) white wine vinegar
300g (10½oz) apples, peeled, cored and cut into 7mm–1cm (⅜–½in) cubes
150g (5½oz) red onions, cut into 7mm–1cm (⅜–½in) cubes
250g (1¼ cups) light brown or muscovado sugar
3 bay leaves
½ tsp mixed spice
1 tsp coriander seeds, lightly crushed
1 tsp mustard seeds, lightly crushed
zest of 1 lemon
1 tsp sea salt

Sterilize your jars and lids (page 212) and make up your spice bag (page 81).

Place everything but the salt into a large, wide, low-sided, heavy-based, non-reactive pan and bring to the boil over a medium-high heat. See page 82 for the process of cooking and jarring, reducing for 30–50 minutes while adding the salt 20 minutes in.

Notes
- If you can't get blackberries or want to make this in a different season, try substituting 1kg (2lb 4oz) plums (stoned and chopped) or 600g (1lb 5oz) cranberries.
- If using frozen berries, defrost first and strain, increasing the cooking time as they retain more liquid than fresh.
- If you are lucky and can get loganberries, tayberries or boysenberries, these work here too.

Sweet and hot tomato chilli jam

I get asked about this recipe a lot. I dedicate the recipe to a Newton & Pott customer of mine, Nadine, who was pretty much addicted to it. She would come by our kitchen in East London for a monthly fix, buying up to 20 jars at a time. I use it with everything from cheese on toast to homemade ramen soup.

Makes 5–6 x 230ml (8fl oz) jars

2kg (4lb 8oz) red tomatoes, blanched
    and skins removed, cored and
    chopped into 5mm (¼in) cubes
2 bay leaves, fresh or dried
30–40g (1–1½oz) red bird's-eye
    chillies or red Thai chillies, stems
    removed and roughly chopped
30g (1oz) fresh root ginger, peeled
    and roughly chopped
20g (¾oz) garlic, roughly chopped
400ml (1¾ cups) cider vinegar
1kg (5 cups) golden or white
    granulated sugar

Sterilize your jars and lids (page 212). Place several small saucers in the freezer.

Place the cubed tomatoes in a large, wide, low-sided, heavy-based, non-reactive pan along with the bay leaves and bring to a simmer, stirring intermittently, warming it through while you prep the rest of the ingredients.

Blitz the chillies, ginger, garlic and half of the vinegar in a blender or food processor for 30 seconds to make a wet paste.

Add the paste to the pan with the remaining vinegar and stir through the sugar until it has dissolved. Increase the heat as high as you can and bring to a vigorous boil – only reduce the heat slightly if it looks as if it will boil over. Stir occasionally.

Thickening can take different times: 20–40 minutes (sometimes more). When it gets glossy and spitty, keep a keener eye on it, stirring more so it doesn't catch and burn. Test when it's ready by using the jam wrinkle test (page 114) – it should be slightly gloopy rather than create a clear wrinkle.

Once ready, ladle into your sterilized jars according to the chutney jarring and storage process (page 82).

Note
- The trick to making this chilli jam great is the chillies you use. Use hot chillies so you get the heat not just the sweet. I find bird's-eye chillies (the very tiny, thin, red ones) are the best to get the heat required. Add more chillies if you want hotter results, or if your chillies aren't very strong. If they are too strong, remove the seeds for less heat and milder results.

New Zealand-style sweetcorn fritters, poached eggs and chutney

In New Zealand, most cafés have sweetcorn fritters on their breakfast/brunch menus, possibly with a poached egg and a bit of chutney. These fritters are something we all grew up making at home from our *Edmonds "Sure to Rise" Cookery Book* (a recipe book that you will find in every Kiwi's kitchen - just ask us). Traditionally, these are made using creamed corn but I've adapted this recipe a bit, as my husband is fussy when it comes to corn from a can.

Serves 2–4 (makes 6–8 fritters)

2–3 corn cobs or 220g (1½ cups) corn kernels (canned is OK)
1–2 Tbsp olive oil (optional)
½ tsp cayenne pepper (optional)
100g (¾ cup) plain (all-purpose) flour
1 tsp baking powder
1 large free-range egg, beaten
70ml (5 Tbsp) milk
3 Tbsp unsweetened Greek yoghurt, soured cream or crème fraîche
large handful of flat-leaf parsley, roughly chopped
1–2 Tbsp vegetable or rapeseed (canola) oil or butter
sea salt and freshly ground black pepper

To serve
2–4 free-range eggs
Green Tomato Chutney (page 84)

Preheat the grill (broiler) to high.

If using corn cobs, rub the kernels with olive oil and season with salt, black pepper and cayenne pepper, if using. If using canned corn kernels, drain and spread out on a baking sheet, then season with salt, pepper and cayenne.

Grill (broil) the cobs for 12–15 minutes, turning every 4–5 minutes, until all the kernels are golden brown with some a little charred. Remove, cool and cut off the kernels using a very sharp knife. If using canned corn, grill for 6–8 minutes, tossing every now and again, until browned.

In a large bowl, sift together the flour and baking powder, lightly season with salt and pepper, and make a well in the middle. Add the beaten egg to the well along with the milk and yoghurt and stir until completely combined. The batter should be thick but loose, like porridge. Mix through the corn and a handful of the chopped parsley, reserving a little parsley for garnish.

Heat the vegetable oil or butter in a large frying pan over a medium heat. Test that it is hot enough by adding a small teaspoon of batter to the pan – when it sizzles, it's ready. Spoon in large tablespoons of the batter in batches. Cook each fritter for 2–3 minutes until small bubbles appear on the top, then flip and cook for a further 2–3 minutes until golden brown.

Poach your eggs – see page 97 for instructions – and serve on top of 2–3 fritters per person. Dollop on a healthy spoonful of chutney, sprinkle with parsley and season generously with salt and pepper.

Notes
- Not just for breakfast, these are great at brunch, lunch or as a dinner treat. Simply leave out the egg and add a fresh leafy salad on the side with a chutney of your choice.
- Add a diced red (bell) pepper, pickled jalapeños, spring onions (scallions) or chillies to the mix for a spicy version.
- Try different chutneys with this recipe that you might have already in your fridge's condiment ghost-town. Traditionally, these go really well with a tomato-based chutney, sauce or relish, but play around with different ones such as red pepper, apple or pear.

Three cheese, rocket and green tomato chutney melt

You don't actually have to go to your local street-food vendor to have the best cheese melt sandwich on the planet. It's easily achieved at home – this is how. I recommend using Cheddar and Red Leicester as the main base cheeses along with another soft melty cheese, but play around with the cheeses you have and find the combination that works best for you.

Serves 2

4 slices of seeded grain bread
1–2 Tbsp unsalted butter, softened
4 heaped tsp Green Tomato Chutney
  (page 84)
40g (1½oz) mature Cheddar cheese,
  cut in thick slices
40g (1½oz) Red Leicester cheese,
  cut in thick slices
40g (1½oz) Provolone, or Raclette
  or Gouda, cut in thick slices
handful of rocket (arugula)
sea salt and freshly ground black
  pepper, to taste

Butter one side of each slice of bread. Start to warm a large iron skillet or non-stick frying pan over a medium heat.

Build the sandwiches, with the buttered side of the bread face down, first with a healthy spread of green tomato chutney, then stack with the cheeses, a liberal seasoning of salt and pepper and lastly add the rocket. Top with a bread slice with the buttered side facing up. Make sure the filling is well within the edges of the bread, so it doesn't ooze out too much while cooking.

Carefully place the sandwiches in the warmed pan, place a sandwich press or another smaller pan on top to press and weigh them down and slowly cook for 5–6 minutes on each side or until golden brown and the cheeses have melted.

Once ready, slice in half and serve hot and gooey.

Notes
- Use any other tomato-based relish or chutney you have to hand. This is quite a forgiving recipe, so experiment with what's in your condiment ghost-town.
- I have also made this with sourdough bread instead of seeded bread.
- Don't be impatient with the timings of this – the trick is to cook slow, not on a super-high heat, to achieve the oozy cheese without burning the bread.

Red lentil dal, gooseberry chutney, raita and wholemeal chapattis

As chutney originates in India, I was lucky to be asked to travel to some of the most remote parts of this incredible country with a CNN Indian film crew to discover its origins. It was fascinating. Chutney-making there is very different from our westernized process, so I had much to learn. This eye-opening experience gave me a new-found appreciation of spice, and this recipe is inspired by the cooks whose homes I visited. I like to add condiments to an Indian curry. I can't seem to shake the desire for the sticky-sweet with spiced dishes, plus a cooling raita and fulfilling chapatti to wrap it all in.

Serves 2–4

Dal
220g (1⅓ cups) red lentils, soaked for 10 minutes, rinsed and drained
1 Tbsp light olive oil or neutral cooking oil
1 bird's-eye chilli, split lengthways, or ½ tsp chilli powder
4 garlic cloves, finely chopped or crushed
15g (½oz) fresh ginger, very finely grated
½ tsp ground turmeric
½ tsp ground coriander
½ tsp ground cumin
3 cloves
1 Tbsp tomato purée (paste)
375g (13oz) ripe tomatoes, finely diced
small handful of coriander (cilantro), roughly chopped
sea salt and freshly ground black pepper

Raita
100g (½ cup) Greek-style yoghurt
squeeze of lemon juice
pinch of sea salt
5–7 fresh mint leaves, roughly chopped
¼ cucumber, diced

To serve
1 Tbsp light olive oil or neutral cooking oil
1 red onion, thinly sliced
wholemeal chapattis (Homemade, page 193)
Gooseberry Chutney (page 84)

Start by preparing the red onion to serve. Heat the oil in a frying pan over a medium–high heat and fry the onion until crispy and browned on the edges. Set aside until ready to serve.

Place the lentils in a saucepan with 1 teaspoon of sea salt and 600ml (2½ cups) water. Cover and bring to the boil, then reduce the heat and simmer with the lid ajar for 7–8 minutes until soft.

Meanwhile, heat the oil in a large saucepan, add the chilli, garlic, ginger, spices and a grinding of black pepper and gently cook for 30 seconds. Stir in the tomato purée and cook for 30 seconds before adding the chopped tomatoes. Stir and cook for 7–8 minutes until reduced.

With a slotted spoon, spoon the lentils into the tomato pan, mixing as you go and adding a little of the lentil cooking water, until the mixture resembles a thick soup. Cover and gently simmer for 15 minutes, removing the lid for the last 5 minutes and stirring through a teaspoon of salt.

Meanwhile, make your chapattis, keeping them warm in a low oven covered with a warm, damp dish towel.

Make the raita by mixing together the yoghurt, lemon juice, salt, mint and cucumber in a small bowl. Set aside until ready to serve.

Plate up the dal, top with the crispy onions and chopped coriander and serve with the gooseberry chutney, raita and chapattis on the side.

Notes
- If you don't have gooseberry chutney, try gooseberry jam. Or, if you are like me, you almost certainly have a jar of mango chutney in your condiment ghost-town that needs using up.
- Try other sweet condiments too, such as Tomato Chilli Jam (page 89) or Green Tomato Chutney (page 84).

Notes
- Traditionally, a kipper is a fat herring that has been butterflied, salt-brined overnight, then cold-smoked. If you can't get them pre-prepared at your local fishmonger, opt for smoked herring or smoked mackerel fillets.
- For an alternative chutney, go for a tart, rich one such as blackberry or cranberry to break up the smokiness of the fish. Failing that, we also like this with green tomato chutney. Or try with pickles, such as sweet pickled gooseberries or blackberries (page 40).

Grilled kippers with brown butter, poached eggs, gooseberry chutney and crème fraîche

My chef friend Oliver Rowe, author of the gorgeously written book *Food for all Seasons*, collaborated with me on a dish we like to call "Kipper & Pickle". Kippers used to be a London cabby's breakfast eaten in the month of January, and are a dish Oliver talks quite fondly about. Oliver's a Londoner, a Camden boy, and me (and I do say this very loosely) the Queen of Pickles. We did a couple of festival demonstrations under this guise – we were almost like a comedy double act. This recipe is an adaptation of the one we came up with for those festivals.

Serves 2

2 kippers or 4 smoked herring fillets
100g (scant ½ cup) salted butter

Poached eggs
pinch of salt
splash of white wine vinegar
2–4 large free-range eggs, at room
    temperature

To serve
crème fraîche
Gooseberry Chutney (page 84)
2 lemon wedges
small handful of flat-leaf parsley,
    roughly chopped (optional)
sea salt and freshly ground black
    pepper

Preheat the grill (broiler) to high.

For the poached eggs, fill a medium saucepan two-thirds full with water. Bring to the boil, add a pinch of salt and a splash of vinegar and reduce the heat to a gentle simmer where you can see bubbles being formed at the bottom and just breaking on the surface of the water.

Meanwhile, put the kippers/herrings on a sheet of foil on a rack and grill (broil) for 2–3 minutes on each side.

Melt the butter in a large frying pan over a medium heat until it starts to bubble. Once the butter starts to turn a light nutty brown, remove from the heat and set aside.

Crack the eggs into individual small cups or ramekins, then drop them into the simmering water one at a time (remember which went in first). Put the timer on for 2 or 3 minutes (depending how soft you prefer your yolk). With a slotted spoon, fish out each egg and place on a plate lined with a clean J-cloth to dry.

While the eggs are cooking, add the grilled kippers to the butter pan, bring it back to a low heat and regularly baste them with the brown butter for about 2 minutes.

Plate the kippers, pouring over the excess butter. Place a poached egg or two on top and a healthy serving of crème fraîche and gooseberry chutney on the side. Squeeze over some lemon juice, sprinkle over the parsley, if using, and season with salt and pepper to taste.

Cranberry, apple and brie sourdough grill with fresh marjoram

Sandwiches are an institution in the UK, and making a good one is down to the ingredients. For me, the key component of a great sandwich has to be what condiment is used, so it becomes a pairing game. I like to think about the balance and try not to overload it with too much, favouring quality over quantity. Classic flavour combinations are good for a reason, so start simple and build from that. I'm always conjuring up ideas to use up the Christmas cranberry sauce; however, this sandwich needs no excuse to.

Makes 1

1 slice of sourdough bread, sliced at the widest part of the loaf, about 17–19cm (6½–7½in) wide
3–4 heaped tsp Cranberry Sauce (page 85)
¼ apple, thinly sliced
90g (3oz) Brie, cut into 3 thick slices
1½ Tbsp pumpkin seeds, lightly toasted
pinch of fresh marjoram leaves
sea salt and freshly ground black pepper, to taste

Preheat the grill (broiler) to high and move the rack to the top shelf.

Toast one side of the bread for a minute or so under the grill, then generously spread the cranberry sauce on the untoasted side. Layer on the apple slices and the chunky slices of cheese, season well with salt and pepper and place under the grill with the oven door ajar for 3–4 minutes, or until the cheese starts to look melty.

Slice in half and sprinkle over the toasted pumpkin seeds and marjoram to serve.

Notes
- Using other rich-flavoured jams you have in your condiment ghost-town also works well. Try it with blackberry, blackcurrant, plum or damson jam or chutney.
- If you can't get fresh marjoram, use dried, or alternatively try rosemary or lemon thyme.

Deep-fried Camembert with cranberry sauce and dukkah

I've chatted and joked a lot with my husband about making a T-shirt with the slogan "Cranberries, not just for Christmas!", so here's a recipe you can eat to enjoy their special flavour all year round. Food has changed a lot since I was little, and my palate has also matured over the years, too. Deep-fried Camembert would be on my birthday dinner wish list as a child. My mother is the inspiration for this classic – and this is one retro dish that I'll never grow out of.

Serves 2–3

1.5–2 litres (6–8 cups) sunflower or rapeseed (canola) oil
2–3 Tbsp plain (all-purpose) flour
1 large free-range egg, lightly whisked
30–40g (⅓–½ cup) regular or panko breadcrumbs (Homemade, page 199)
1 whole Camembert wheel, chilled

To serve
Cranberry Sauce (page 85)
Dukkah (page 210)

Fill a deep heavy-based saucepan or a deep-fat fryer with oil to a depth of 6cm (2½in) and heat to 190°C (375°F), or until a chunk of bread dropped in browns in 30 seconds. Take care, as hot oil can be very dangerous if left unattended.

Put the flour, egg and breadcrumbs onto separate small plates. Cut the Camembert into 6 wedges, then coat each edge first in flour, then in egg, then toss in the breadcrumbs until well coated.

With a slotted spoon, carefully lower 3 wedges at a time into the hot oil. Let them sizzle away until they go a lovely golden brown, about 2–3 minutes. Remove with the slotted spoon, draining off the excess oil, and place onto paper towels. Repeat with the last 3 wedges, keeping the fried ones in a warm oven until ready to serve, if necessary.

Warm through the cranberry sauce in a small saucepan over a low heat for about 5 minutes.

Serve the wedges warm with the warm cranberry sauce on the side and a sprinkle of dukkah.

Note
- Alternative jams, such as redcurrant, blackcurrant or gooseberry will also work well. Or try a rich berry or plum chutney instead of the cranberry.

Chicken liver pâté with blackberry and apple chutney and brioche toast

I got the lovely opportunity to collaborate with the Fodder gang, a London-based, uber-talented group of four people creating amazing food and dining experiences that culinary dreams are made of. I'd never worked with a professional chef quite like Michael Thompson before; he's worked in Simon Rogan's kitchen. I'm self-taught but I've worked in a lot of kitchens over the years and my willingness to absorb, get stuck in and learn is never-ending. It was an amazing experience and I would do it all over again. We wanted to combine my preserving knowledge with Michael's all-round culinary expertise, so one of the dishes we created was a PBJ: pâté, brioche, jam. This recipe is my chutney version.

Serves 2 (makes about 200g/7oz pâté)

80g (⅓ cup) unsalted butter
2 Tbsp olive oil
1 large onion, finely diced
1–2 garlic cloves, finely chopped
2 bay leaves
250g (9oz) free-range chicken livers, trimmed and roughly chopped
40ml (scant 3 Tbsp) brandy
sea salt and freshly ground black pepper

To serve

4 thick slices of brioche or milk bread loaf (Homemade, page 198)
butter, for frying
Blackberry and Apple Chutney (page 86)

Melt the butter and oil in a medium frying pan over a medium heat. Add the onion and season very generously, then gently sauté for 4–5 minutes until soft and translucent but not browned. Add the garlic and bay leaves and cook for 30 seconds, then add the livers and sauté, stirring intermittently, for 6–8 minutes until they look almost cooked through. Stir in the brandy, increase the heat slightly and simmer for a further 2–3 minutes until you see the first signs of sticking to the pan. Remove from the heat and let cool slightly.

Remove the bay leaves and blend the mixture in a food processor until completely smooth, tasting and seasoning as you go. Strain/push through a fine-mesh sieve if you want your pâté extra smooth, otherwise scrape into a 250ml (8½fl oz) dish with a spatula. Cool, cover and store in the fridge.

For the PBJ sandwich, toast each side of the slices of brioche in a frying pan with a little butter until golden. Spread a thick layer of pâté on 2 slices of brioche and a thick layer of chutney or jam on the other 2 and sandwich them together. Cut off the crusts with a sharp knife and cut in half to serve.

Notes
- If you don't want to make a PBJ sandwich, just serve the liver pâté with seeded toasts and a side of chutney or marmalade.
- Use other jams you have tucked away in your condiment ghost-town, such as raspberry, rhubarb or a marmalade. You'll be surprised what works.
- For a bit of drama, clarify some butter, pour on top of the pâté and set a bay or sage leaf into it before cooling in the fridge.
- Make a vegetarian version by replacing the livers with 400g (14oz) sliced button or chestnut (cremini) mushrooms.

Notes
- Instead of pork, use minced (ground) chicken or turkey, finely chopped mushrooms or shellfish.
- The Savoy cabbage can be replaced with spring greens, napa or white cabbage, kale, cavolo nero or even kimchi (squeezed and unsalted).
- Substitute the tomato chilli jam by simply mixing fish sauce with sesame oil and a chopped chilli, or use the sweet chilli sauce you have stashed away on your condiment ghost-town shelf.

Pork and cabbage dumplings with tomato chilli dipping sauce

This recipe can be adapted to be vegan, vegetarian or pescatarian – just substitute any variety of Asian-style mushroom, such as king oyster or shiitake, with tofu, or try king prawns (jumbo shrimp). If you're feeling really fancy, try scallops or lobster.

Makes 25–30

2–3 outer Savoy cabbage leaves, hard vein removed, very finely shredded
2 tsp sea salt
1 Tbsp vegetable oil
1 small banana shallot, finely diced
1 large king oyster, oyster or shiitake mushroom, finely diced
5cm (2in) piece of fresh root ginger, peeled and finely minced or chopped
bunch of coriander (cilantro), finely chopped
200g (7oz) good-quality minced (ground) pork
1 large free-range egg
½ Tbsp sesame oil
1½ Tbsp soy sauce
1 packet round gyoza wrappers (Homemade, page 202), defrosted if frozen
plain (all-purpose) flour, for dusting
1 Tbsp sunflower or rapeseed (canola) oil, for cooking

Tomato chilli dipping sauce
4–5 Tbsp Tomato Chilli Jam (page 89)
1–2 Tbsp water

Place the sliced cabbage in a bowl, sprinkle with the salt, then mix through, cover and set aside for 15 minutes.

Heat the vegetable oil in a frying pan over a medium heat, add the shallot and mushroom and fry for 4–5 minutes. Transfer to a large bowl, stir through the ginger and coriander, then add the meat and mix until well combined. Whisk the egg with the sesame oil and soy sauce and stir through. Squeeze the cabbage with your hands, removing any excess liquid, then mix it through the meat mixture with your hands until everything is well combined. Cover and refrigerate for 30 minutes.

Create a wrapping station with the pile of gyoza wrappers, a small bowl of water and a tray lightly dusted with flour. Work with 3–4 wrappers at a time. Place a healthy teaspoonful of filling into the middle of each wrapper, wet the outer edge of each wrapper with a little water and fold in half, firmly sealing the edges from the middle outwards, to form semi-circles. Pinch, crimp and fold 4 or 5 pleats along the curved edge of each dumpling, securing any openings. Place each dumpling on the floured tray and continue filling. If you can't master the pleat, then just keep them as sealed semi-circles.

You can freeze them at this point, if wished. To freeze, place the tray in the freezer and when they are completely frozen gather them up into a freezer bag. They will keep like this for 3–4 months.

To cook, heat a frying pan until hot. Add the cooking oil to the pan, then place as many dumplings in the pan as will fit without them touching. Fry for 1–2 minutes on each side until browned, quickly splash in a dash of water, about 2 tablespoons, and immediately cover the pan with a lid. Steam for 3–4 minutes. If cooking from frozen, add an extra 3–4 minutes to the steaming time.

Serve with a dipping sauce of tomato chilli jam mixed with a little water.

Sweet chilli chicken wings with kimchi fried rice

When I was young, my mum would make us the best marinated chicken nibblets. I still ask for them when I return to New Zealand for a visit (although I just heard she cheats nowadays and gets the butcher to do it). As a child, I always thought that I was eating little baby chickens and it wasn't until I was older that I learned that they were really chicken wings that had been cut at the joint. I think my mum took a small sadistic joy from the fact that we thought she was feeding us sweet little chicks.

Serves 2

5 Tbsp Tomato Chilli Jam (page 89)
1 Tbsp water
1 Tbsp sesame oil
1 tsp sea salt
1 Tbsp soy sauce
6 chicken wings or 12 jointed wings
2 spring onions (scallions), finely
    chopped
1 Tbsp sesame seeds
Kimchi Fried Rice (page 76, omitting
    the fried eggs)
bunch of coriander (cilantro), roughly
    chopped

The night before, or in the morning before you start your day, mix up the tomato chilli jam in a bowl with the water, sesame oil, salt and soy sauce. Throw in your chicken wings and massage with the marinade until they are completely coated. Cover with waxed paper or a towel and place in the fridge to marinate for at least 8–24 hours.

When ready to cook, preheat the oven to 220°C (200°C fan/425°F/gas mark 7).

Remove the chicken wings from the fridge and massage again with your hands before placing them on a shallow baking sheet so they are not overlapping each other. Cover each one with any remaining marinade from the bowl and sprinkle with the chopped spring onions. Bake in the hot oven for 10–15 minutes, then turn them, sprinkle with the sesame seeds and cook for a further 10–15 minutes or until the sauce has started to get sticky and gooey.

During the second half of cooking, start making your kimchi fried rice.

Remove the wings from the oven and allow to cool for 5 minutes before serving on top of your kimchi fried rice with a scattering of coriander.

Notes
- Instead of tomato chilli jam, you can use any sweet chilli sauce substitute you might already have lurking on the condiment shelf of the fridge.
- If you are a vegan, vegetarian or pescatarian, substitute the chicken with tofu, tempeh, jackfruit or prawns (shrimp). Cooking times may vary.
- Double or triple this recipe if you have more mouths to feed or want to take them to a pot-luck party (without the kimchi rice).

Sweet

Jam, marmalade and jelly

Jam, marmalade and jelly are the hardest of all of the preserves to get right. I think everyone believes that if their grandmother used to make it, how hard can it actually be. However, our grandmas used to match fruit measurements to sugar measurements (which is bound to make anything set) and today we are a lot more conscious of our sugar intake.

So, how do we achieve a set? We rely on a chemical reaction from the natural setting element that is present in a lot of fruit (less so in vegetables) called pectin. Pectin starts to release from the fruit when heated, and when combined with acid (also found in most fruits) it starts to congeal and gel up. The tricky thing is that all fruit comes with different levels of pectin and acid so it takes a bit of knowledge and work to perfect the ideal set.

Not all jams set the same – there are what I like to refer to as "soft-sets" and "hard-sets". Fruits that are high in pectin and acid will tend to create a firmer set, whereas fruits that are low in pectin and acid create a softer, looser set. Both are great and have different uses when added to different dishes. Keep referring to the pectin/acid chart I've provided (page 115) to guide you when you start out.

Jams are predominantly fruit with texture, where the fruit is chopped and cooked down a little into pulp before sugar is added, sometimes containing whole fruit chunks. Marmalades, although traditionally made from quinces, tend to be made from citrus fruits – the flesh and rind are softened down with a lot of water, then sugar is added to create a set. In jellies, we extract the fruit juice from the fibre, discard the pulp and set this remaining juice with sugar.

There are many different ways to make jam, marmalade and jelly. The following methods are how I have got the best results making it over ten years, but different preservers may give you different advice on techniques. Do what feels most natural to you and where you get the most successful results. My way is to cook as fast as I can over very high heats to release the pectin for a quicker set. The longer you cook the fruit the more it turns into fruit sugars. Shorter cooking times mean I get more of the natural vitamins and flavour from the fruit into my jam without increasing the fructose levels, where low- or no-sugar jams have to cook longer to achieve a set, therefore increasing these levels.

The following pages are a guide to teach you ways of adding flavour combinations to your jams and marmalades. Each preserving recipe introduces a new flavour addition, from herbs, florals, nuts or spices, to alcohol or other flavoured liquids. These aim to give you inspiration on how these different flavours can be added, but feel free to mix and match fruit to flavour additions to suit your own ideas.

Produce

Always use firm, fresh fruits, as these are higher in pectin. The riper fruits are, the more they lose their pectin content. Always wash, then hull, peel, zest, slice and chop, cutting out any browning bits or discarding any unsavoury ones. Mix high-pectin/acid fruits with lower ones to get a firmer set. See page 115 for my pectin/acid chart.

Sugars

Fruit and sugar are the main ingredients in jam. You may be shocked when you actually measure the sugar out, as it looks like a lot. However, you don't eat jam like you might a cake or a soft drink; it's eaten in smaller quantities, maybe a teaspoon to a tablespoon at a time, so your actual sugar intake might not be as large as eating a whole blueberry muffin.

I tend to use white granulated or white caster sugar, as I want purity of flavour and for the fruit to be the hero. You can use alternative sugars, but this isn't the way I make jam and you would have to do your own experiments. I find alternatives can sometimes add different flavours that I don't want.

You can buy jam sugar and preserving sugar – these can be helpful to assist the setting process. Jam sugar is ordinary white sugar with added powdered pectin and acidity. Use jam sugar if you want a firmer set on your lower-pectin fruits (see chart on page 115) such as strawberries and rhubarb. Preserving sugar has a larger granule, making it great for making marmalades as it dissolves quicker, giving a clearer appearance for your suspended citrus peel.

Pectin

Pectin is naturally contained in all fruit and vegetables, but the levels differ in each fruit, so do refer to page 115 to guide you in your process. If a fruit is low in pectin, you can add another fruit that has a higher content to help the set. You can also add commercial pectins and I sometimes rely on a rapid-set powdered pectin or jam sugar if I need the extra help. These are natural products, where the pectin and acid are extracted from lemon rinds and pips, which are high in both elements. If using powdered pectin, always mix it through the sugar first.

Acid levels

These also differ from fruit to fruit (see chart on page 115). I usually add a bit of lemon juice to balance this. Adjust the measure of freshly squeezed lemon juice according to the fruit you are using. Commercial jams might use citrus acid here, but go natural for your homemade jam.

Equipment

- A large, wide, heavy-based, low-sided pan is essential. Jam pans or Mason pans are the best, as the angled sides create a condensed heat source at the bottom with a wider surface area for the heat to escape, allowing your jams to cook quickly at high temperatures.
- Jars and lids that you can sterilize – used jars and lids are suitable, providing they are in good condition, don't have chips or cracks and the lid seals are intact. Make sure when buying new jars and lids to buy good-quality ones that can withstand high heat.
- Digital sugar thermometer, if preferred, for reaching high temperatures
- A long-handled wooden spoon
- A wide-mouthed funnel
- A spatula
- A heat-safe measuring jug
- A ladle
- Large muslin (cheesecloth) squares for making/hanging jellies

Jam process

Place several small saucers in the freezer at least 1 hour before you start. Always begin by sterilizing your jars and lids (page 212) and use them straight from the oven.

Wash, peel, core (where needed) and cut your fruit into bite-sized pieces, about 1cm (½in) cubes, leaving berries whole (if not too large). Heat and soften the fruit first, until it becomes pulp. For whole chunky bits in your jam, keep some fruit pieces aside for later in the process. Add the recipe's water measurement and the lemon juice to help it soften. If using frozen fruit, defrost it first and don't add the water, as it retains a lot in the freezing process. Only stir now and again at this stage, so it doesn't stick to the bottom of the pan. Different fruits are stickier, so be vigilant and never walk away from your jam.

When it is pulpy and bubbling, add the sugar, stirring until it has completely dissolved. Add any of the extra whole or chunks of fruit here, so they don't break down as much. Turn up the heat to the highest setting, and only stir intermittently, not allowing too much cold air into the mix. There's a fine line between stirring to ensure it's not catching and burning and stirring too much and lowering its temperature. Ideally, you want the jam to get to a temperature of 104°C (220°F).

I find thermometers unreliable, so to judge when my jam is ready for set/wrinkle testing and jarring (page 114), I boil it on the highest heat until the rolling bubbles thicken, becoming slower and ploppier. This is the heat struggling to break through to the surface as the density of the jam becomes thicker and "jams up". Timings always differ, depending on the fruit pectin levels (page 115), the pan you are using, and the heat source – even the temperature of the room can affect your timings – so use your eyes and instinct to make a judgement.

Jams can be stored in a cool, dark place for up to 6-12 months. Once opened, store in the fridge and eat within 4-6 weeks.

Marmalade process

Place several small saucers in the freezer at least 1 hour before you start. Always begin by sterilizing your jars and lids (page 212) and use them straight from the oven.

Wash and prep your citrus. When using oranges, take half the amount and carefully remove the skin first by cutting off the top and the bottom with a very sharp knife. Sit the orange on a cut end and carefully slice off the skin. Try not to take off too much flesh but at the same time remove as much white pith as possible. Do this with the total amount if using grapefruit, as they tend to have a thick white pith.

Lay the skins flat, white sides up, and remove as much of the pith as you can with a very sharp knife, much like separating the skin from a fish. Use this cleaned peel to make zest to add to your marmalade by slicing it into long, thin, super-fine strips, 1mm (⅛₂in) wide.

Chop the flesh of the peeled oranges and grapefruit into small cubes, about 5mm-1cm (¼-½in) in size, removing the pips as you go and as much of the membrane inside as you can. Cut the other half of the unpeeled oranges in half lengthways and slice very finely with a sharp

knife into 5mm-1cm (¼-½in) semi-circles. Do this with all the fruit if the citrus has thinner skin and white pith, like clementines, limes and some lemons. If you like less skin in your marmalade, then use more of the cut flesh and less of the cut skin.

Place all of the prepped peel, flesh and semi-circles into a large jam pan with as much of the juice collected on your board while chopping. Add the water and lemon juice and any spices, according to the recipe. Boil on the highest heat, stirring intermittently, for 20-25 minutes, until it has reduced a bit and the peel has softened.

If adding vanilla, mix the seeds through the sugar first, with a fork, for an even distribution, and add the pod. Add the sugar to the pan and stir until it has completely dissolved. Bring back to a rapid boil, then boil for a further 15-30 minutes, stirring intermittently so it doesn't catch and burn. Keep your marmalade on the highest heat on the largest heat element to achieve the best set. If it looks like it might boil over, reduce the heat slightly to regain control, but you want it boiling rapidly, so don't be tempted to reduce the heat for too long.

When it starts to look syrupy and heavier, it's time to set test/wrinkle test to judge if it's ready for jarring (page 114). Marmalades can be stored in a cool, dark place for up to 12-18 months. Once opened, store in the fridge and eat within 6-8 weeks.

Set test/wrinkle test and jarring

I find this the most reliable way to tell if the jam, marmalade or jelly is at the desired set: "hard set" for jelly and some jams and marmalades - with high pectin/acid levels; and "soft set" for other jams and marmalades with lower pectin/acid levels.

When ready to test, remove the pan from the heat, take one of the saucers from the freezer, drop ¼ teaspoon of jam onto the frozen saucer and place in the fridge for 1 minute. This mimics the cooling process. Remove the saucer and gently push the jam, marmalade or jelly with your finger. There should be a hard or soft wrinkle on the surface for a hard or soft set. Not all fruits will ever make it to a hard set, creating a prominent wrinkle. So with a soft set, scoop it up with the forefinger and allow it to drip off - you'll want a slow drip. If not at the desired set, return to the heat and test again until it is.

If ready, skim off any foam and stir through any flavourings (if not added at the beginning). Ladle the hot jam, marmalade or jelly into hot sterilized jars through a wide-mouthed funnel or pour from a heat-proof jug, filling the jars to 2-3mm (⅛in) from the top. Clean the rim with a damp cloth and seal immediately with a hot sterilized lid. This needs to be a speedy process so you don't lose too much heat from the jam or the jar. Seal everything immediately so that bacteria can't survive in the high temperatures. Once cooled, date and label.

Some preservers use a canning bath to heat process after sealing. Here the filled, sealed jars are brought to a gentle boil in a pan of water, covered entirely, for 10-15 minutes. This ensures that no bacteria will survive and can add to the longevity but at the risk of overcooking. Try undersetting your jam first if using this process. I never do this, as if you seal promptly without losing too much temperature this should be enough for a secure environment.

Troubleshooting

If you have a little jam, jelly or marmalade left in your pot after jarring, not enough to fill a whole jar, then put this into a heat-safe Tupperware or smaller jar and keep in the fridge once cooled. Eat this one first.

Sometimes, you'll get some foam or "jam scum" while cooking. These are little white bubbles that form around the edges of the pan. This is fine, it's just the foam of any impurities rising to the surface and can be easily and carefully scooped off with a spatula or spoon. Some stir through a knob of butter at the end to dissolve it, but it then wouldn't be plant-based.

If you find mould when you first open a jar it means it wasn't sterilized or sealed properly. Make sure you always fill hot jam into hot sterilized jars and seal with hot lids - all around 100°C (212°F) - and this shouldn't happen. If it still happens, upgrade your jars and/or lids. All lids these days have a rubber seal inside that forms itself around the rim of the jar to create a secure seal. Make sure these haven't deteriorated. If all else fails, use a disc of baking paper to line the surface of the jam before sealing or go old-school and use wax paraffin.

You can reset a loose jam/marmalade by decanting and re-boiling it with a little more sugar mixed with powdered pectin and lemon juice.

However, it can start to caramelize and darken in colour. If your set is too hard when you come to eat it, just mix in a little water to loosen it. In this case, it will have to be eaten quickly, as adding water has exposed it to live bacteria.

If you're struggling to get a good set with your jam, marmalade or jelly, try substituting the sugar you're using with a jam or preserving sugar – see sugars (page 111).

Pectin/acid chart

	Pectin levels			Acid levels		
	High	Medium	Low	High	Medium	Low
Blackcurrants	●			●		
Crab apples	●			●		
Cranberries	●				●	
Gooseberries	●			●		
Plums (unripe)	●			●		
Quinces	●			●	●	
Currants	●			●		
Citrus fruits	●			●	●	
Cooking apples	●	●		●	●	
Apricots		●			●	
Grapes (unripe)		●			●	
Logan berries		●			●	
Medlars		●				●
Plums (ripe)		●			●	
Blackberries		●	●		●	●
Blueberries		●	●			●
Cherries			●			●
Figs			●			●
Grapes (ripe)			●			●
Melons			●			●
Nectarines			●			●
Peaches			●			●
Pears			●			●
Rhubarb			●	●		
Strawberries			●			●

Adding alcohol

Alcohol in jam makes for lovely boozy infusions of flavours. Adding alcohol at the end of cooking when the temperature is slightly over 100°C (212°F) ensures the alcohol evaporates, leaving behind only the essence, the flavour of the liquor used. You will see it rapidly bubble when you pour it in as the alcohol reacts to the heat and "burns off". These jams are therefore safe for children to enjoy.

Flavour pairing is the fun bit. In the recipe on page 124, I've used Cointreau to achieve an orange bitter-sweet balance matched with the overly sweet figs in my jam. Although I have kept this a very classic flavour profile – figs and orange – don't let this limit you. Play around with a variety of different alcohols that may be more suited to your palate. Whisky or mezcal can be nice additions as well, bringing a lovely smoky taste, while Campari or Cynar bring bitter tones, amaretto and Frangelico are nutty, and gin or amaro are botanical.

Adding nibs, beans and kernels

Cacao nibs and ground coffee beans have been friends to bakers for a long time and are also a really lovely addition to jams. Cacao nibs bring a nice bitter chocolate flavour. Pairing chocolate and fruit has been a classic match, so why not add them to your preserves as you might when cooking. Try with pears, raspberries or strawberries. I like bitter chocolate with apricots (see page 123).

If you're not a fan of bitter cacao notes but love coffee, try stirring a teaspoon of roughly ground coffee beans just before jarring instead of the cacao nibs. Coffee brings a rich, bitter caramel flavour to the jam and you can experiment with different coffee blends to create different flavour notes (although they may discolour the fruits' hue).

Another addition worth mentioning, as I have seen jam recipes using them, is the kernels from the stones/pips of stone fruit, such as apricots, cherries, peaches, plums and nectarines. Simply get a hammer and crack them open to find the treasure inside. Kernels do have a great nutty flavour and they are a lovely way to use your fruit "nose-to-tail", but do proceed with caution as the kernels contain amygdalin, which the body can turn into cyanide if too many are consumed. I usually steer clear, just in case.

Adding herbs or leaves

With fresh herbs or leaves that are softer in texture, such as mint, verbena and basil, I tend to macerate the prepped fruit and a little of the sugar mixed in with the chopped herbs. Place in a covered bowl in the fridge for at least 6–8 hours or overnight to infuse. Do this for the peach and mint jam recipe (page 123). If the leaves are extra-large, such as fig or grape leaves, just tear them up and mix them through.

If the herbs or leaves are tougher in texture, such as rosemary, thyme or lemon thyme, I add these, finely chopped or plucked, when the jam is ready, just after skimming off any foam. Alternatively, try tying them up in a tight bunch and let them infuse in the jam while cooking, and fish them out at the end.

If you are using dried herbs or leaves, these are sometimes better brewed up as a tea first (page 119), to release their flavour into the jam.

Try mint, lemon balm, rosemary, thyme, lemon thyme, sage, basil, bay leaves, lemon verbena, marjoram, fig leaves or lime leaves. Or go wild, literally: go and forage in the countryside or grow these in your garden. You can experiment with other foraged leaves, such as peach, plum or cherry, but I find they sometimes lack the punchy flavours that you need to penetrate the fruit to do them any justice in a jam, so try to stick to the more fragrant ones.

Combining seasonal fruits

Another idea is to match a bunch of fruits that are in season together. If you decide to go berry picking (a fun thing to do with the kids) it works really well to bunch all the different berries together in one jam.

Although rhubarb isn't technically a fruit, it does make great jam. Try pairing it with berries or citrus fruits; due to rhubarb lacking pectin,

these additional fruits will help to create a firmer set. Or try mixing up citrus fruits in a marmalade (see Rainbow Marmalade on page 128), using all the different rinds and flesh to add colour and multiple flavours for your palate.

Work with the seasons to your advantage where you can, but if you find you have a surplus of berries, freeze them to use with another fruit at a later date. After defrosting, just omit any water listed in the recipe.

Jam is sweet, so think about combining the tarter fruits together, such as strawberry and gooseberry (see page 125). The sugar in the recipe brings the sweeter element while remaining true to the sharpness of both fruits. Strawberries are not high in pectin, but gooseberries are, so mixing the two aids the set of your jam.

Adding nuts

Adding nuts provides a bit of texture to your jam, and of course the nutty flavour when you bite into one. When adding, try to think about the flavour balance and how you are pairing the fruit with the nut.

I like flaked (slivered) almonds as they have a nice, subtle, nutty flavour and, being a jam purist, I like the fruit to be the star – it's the reason we are making jam, right? However, sometimes, as in baking, it's nice to add a different complexity or flavour to the mix, so stronger nuts like hazelnuts, walnuts and cobnuts are also a great addition.

You can toast the nuts, which enriches their flavour and releases the natural oils, but make sure you rest and pat them dry, as the oils can mess with the preservation of your jam. Make sure the nuts aren't pre-salted and roughly chop if they aren't already.

In the recipe on page 125, I pair hazelnuts with blackberries. Unlike most people, I'm not a fan of hazelnuts and chocolate, however I adore them paired with creamier or sharper flavours, hence the blackberries. Work with your own palate and discover what works best for you.

Adding florals

Some florals can have a strong impact in jams, notably with subtle fruits like apple, pear or apricot, so be gentle and proceed with caution – you don't want an addition of lavender to end up tasting like your grandma's knicker drawer. Play around with the floral's strength – sometimes just the suggestion of their flavour is nice. Work with different measurements to get the right flavour for you and think about the pairings and how one might dominate another when making your jam.

There are a couple of ways of adding florals to your jam, marmalade and jelly. If using dried edible flowers, such as dried hibiscus (see Rhubarb and Hibiscus Jam on page 122) or chamomile, you can make a strong infused tea with the florals (page 120). Add this brew (strained or not) at the beginning of the cooking process in place of any water measurement in the recipe.

Alternatively - when using very potent dried florals, like lavender - stir them directly in at the end of cooking, after you have skimmed off any foam. If the dried petals are more subtle in flavour, such as dried rose, you can try adding some extract to enhance their aroma.

With fresh flowers, such as foraged elderflower, meadowsweet, rose petals or lilac, macerate them with the chopped fruit overnight, with half of the sugar quantity, to allow the flavours to penetrate the fruit before cooking the next day.

Adding cordials, syrups, extracts and teas

Different flavoured liquids can be added to the fruit to enhance your jam, marmalades or jellies. When adding, think about flavours that match each other: some might be classic combinations, like raspberry and elderflower; others may work when you think they might not. There are a variety of cordials, syrups, extracts and teas available to play around with in your jam. Be adventurous with different ones.

If using a cordial like in the Raspberry and Elderflower Jam (page 124), add it at the end, after skimming off any foam, so that the flavour doesn't burn out while cooking. If using extracts, you'll find these a much stronger and more concentrated flavour, so add 1-2 teaspoons to begin with, and make a note if you need more or less for the next time.

If adding tea, then make up a strong brew with about 100-150ml (⅓-⅔ cup) rested boiling water and omit any additional water listed in the recipe. Add this at the beginning of cooking, so while softening and pulping the fruit.

Adding spices

When using spices in jams, marmalades and jellies, I like to use the ones that are associated with baking with the exception of wanting a little fire in the flavour. Play around with the vast array of spices available at your disposal, sticking to things like cardamom, star anise, cinnamon, nutmeg, ginger (ground and freshly grated), mixed spice or allspice, cloves, mace, saffron, vanilla seeds, juniper berries, fennel, caraway, poppy or nigella seeds. For a touch of heat, use spices such as chilli flakes or roughly ground pink, white or black peppercorns but don't go too wild with heat - it could cancel out your fruit flavour.

Spices can be added whole at the beginning of cooking, but if you won't want to bite into them when eating, remove them at the end, just before jarring. Alternatively, lightly crush or muddle them to release the fragrance or grind into a fine powder and mix this through the sugar. before adding to the softened fruit.

Think about your fruit/spice pairings, and what you think make good matches. Classic combinations are classic for a reason, like the Lemon and Poppy-seed Marmalade (page 129) - they work well. But have fun and experiment with new pairings and see what works best for you.

Some fruits such as pears and apples make for a milder jam, which can sometimes seem a little too close to baby food. By adding a spice this livens them up, like in my Pear and Cardamom Jam (page 122), making it more adult.

Rhubarb and hibiscus jam

Makes 6–7 x 250ml (8½fl oz) jars

30g (1oz) dried edible hibiscus
  flowers, infused for 10 minutes in
  200ml (generous ¾ cup) boiled
  water, then strained, reserving
  the liquid
1.4kg (3lb) rhubarb, forced or field
  (defrosted if frozen), chopped
  into 1–2cm (½–¾in) pieces
50ml (3½ Tbsp) freshly squeezed
  lemon juice
700g (3½ cups) white granulated
  sugar

For method: see the jam process on page 112 with notes below, for adding florals see page 119, and for set-testing and jarring see page 114.

Notes
- Rhubarb tends to want to stick to the bottom of the pan, so be vigilant with stirring, mostly at the beginning while softening to a pulp. It is high in acidity but not in pectin, so you will generally always get a soft-set, loose jam.
- Play around with the different floral measurements – some are stronger in taste than others, so experiment to get the potency you like. For stronger flavours, you may want to add matching extracts, such as violet essence or rose water, or to mimic the floral used.

Pear and cardamom jam

Makes 4–5 x 250ml (8½fl oz) jars

2kg (4lb 8oz) firm pears, peeled and
  cored: 1.2kg puréed; 800g cut
  into 5mm (¼in) cubes
2 Tbsp water
40ml (2½ Tbsp) freshly squeezed
  lemon juice
4 green cardamom pods, lightly
  smashed
850g (4¼ cups) white granulated
  sugar

For method: see the jam process on page 112 with notes below, for adding spices see page 120, and for set-testing and jarring see page 114.

Notes
- Add the cardamom pods to the puréed pear with the lemon juice and bring to a boil before adding and dissolving the sugar, then add the cubed pear (so these chunks don't break down and add texture).
- Remove the cardamom pods when ready to jar, if desired.
- Pears are low in pectin and acidity, so this will always be a loose jam. If you want a slightly firmer set, try using jam sugar, add powdered pectin to plain sugar or use a liquid pectin.
- Substitute pears for apples – apples are higher in pectin and acid so will give a firmer set.
- Try a different matching of spices, such as 1 teaspoon of fennel seeds, added at the end just before jarring, or 1 whole cinnamon stick added at the beginning, infusing while cooking, then plucked out before jarring.

Apricot and cacao nib jam

Makes 4–5 x 250ml (8½fl oz) jars

1.3kg (2lb 14oz) apricots, stoned
    (pitted) and chopped into 1cm
    (½in) cubes (1kg/2lb 4oz flesh)
140ml (scant ⅔ cup) water
50ml (3½ Tbsp) freshly squeezed
    lemon juice
550g (2¾ cups) white granulated
    sugar
1 Tbsp cacao nibs

For method: see the jam process on page 112 with notes below, for adding nibs see page 116, and for set-testing and jarring see page 114.

Notes
- Apricots tend to stick to the bottom of the pan, so be vigilant with stirring mostly at the beginning while softening to a pulp and before adding the sugar.
- Stir through the cacao nibs after skimming off any foam from the jam and just before jarring.
- Apricots are medium in acidity and pectin, so the set will be a bit firmer than a peach or a pear jam; the set will be heavy and loose unless you use commercial natural pectins or jam sugar.

Peach and mint jam

Makes 5–6 x 250ml (8½fl oz) jars

1.9kg (4lb 4oz) ripe but firm peaches,
    pitted and chopped into 1cm
    (½in) pieces (1.4kg/3lb flesh)
10–15g (⅓–½oz) mint leaves, washed
    and roughly chopped
800g (4 cups) white granulated
    sugar
60ml (¼ cup) freshly squeezed
    lemon juice

For method: see the jam process on page 112 with notes below, for adding herbs see page 116, and for set-testing and jarring see page 114.

Notes
- At least 8-12 hours before cooking, prep the fruit and mix in the mint and half of the sugar, cover and refrigerate to macerate.
- Peaches are low in pectin and acidity so this will always be a soft-set, loose jam – don't expect it to firm up.
- This recipe works with all stone fruits, so try nectarines, plums, cherries, apricots or loquat. You can choose to remove the skins of the fruit or not. Also, try this with berries. See page 115 for their different pectin/acid levels.

Raspberry and elderflower jam

Makes 4–5 x 250ml (8½fl oz) jars

900g (2lb) raspberries, fresh or
 frozen
40ml (2½ Tbsp) water
30ml (2 Tbsp) freshly squeezed
 lemon juice
500g (2½ cups) white granulated
 sugar
80ml (scant ⅓ cup) elderflower
 cordial or syrup

For method: see the jam process on page 112 with notes below, for adding cordial/syrup see page 120, and for set-testing and jarring see page 114.

Notes
- If using frozen berries, make sure they are defrosted first and omit the listed water.
- Always stir through the cordial, extract or essence at the end of the process, after skimming off the foam and before jarring.
- Raspberries are medium in pectin and acidity making for a firmer set. Don't overcook your jam if you like a softer texture.
- Try using rosehip syrup, rose extract, orange blossom cordial, ginger cordial, Earl Grey tea, chamomile tea, lemon verbena tea, yuzu cordial, lemongrass syrup, hazelnut syrup, vanilla extract, rose extract or almond extract.
- Try different fruit jam combinations, such as gooseberry and chamomile tea, leaving in some of the flowers; raspberry and rose; blackberry and yuzu; plum and lemongrass.

Fig and Cointreau jam

Makes 5–6 x 250ml (8½fl oz) jars

1.25kg (2lb 12oz) ripe figs, green or
 black, cut into 1cm (½in) pieces
90ml (⅓ cup) water
40ml (2½ Tbsp) freshly squeezed
 lemon juice
750g (3¾ cups) white granulated
 sugar
100ml (generous ⅓ cup) Cointreau,
 Grand Marnier or Campari

For method: see the jam process on page 112 with notes below, for adding alcohol see page 116, and for set-testing and jarring see page 114.

Notes
- Always stir through the alcohol at the end of the process, after skimming off the foam and before jarring.
- Figs are high in pectin and acidity, so need less cooking time to get to a firmer set. They are also less juicy so tend to need more water to soften them into a pulp at the beginning.
- Try to match your flavour profiles of fruit to alcohol. Suggestions: marmalades with smoky whiskies or mezcal; strawberries or raspberries with strong herby botanicals like Pimm's or gin; apricots with nutty suggestions like amaretto or Frangelico; apples with rum; peaches with dry vermouth; pears with brandy.

Blackberry and hazelnut jam

Makes about 4 x 250ml (8½fl oz) jars

1.25kg (2lb 12oz) blackberries, fresh or frozen
40ml (2½ Tbsp) water
30ml (2 Tbsp) freshly squeezed lemon juice
600g (3 cups) white granulated sugar
50g (⅓ cup) hazelnuts, roughly chopped

For method: see the jam process on page 112 with notes below, for adding nuts see page 119, and for set-testing and jarring see page 114.

Notes
- If using frozen berries, make sure they are defrosted first and omit the listed water.
- Always stir through the prepped nuts straight after the sugar has dissolved, enabling them to get to the heat required for a sterile environment in your jar.
- Other fruit/nut ideas: apricot and flaked almonds; plum and cobnuts; gooseberry and walnuts; raspberry and chopped almonds; mango and cashews; blackberry and Brazil nuts; peach and pecans.

Strawberry and gooseberry jam

Makes 5–6 x 250ml (8½fl oz) jars

600g (1lb 5oz) strawberries, hulled and halved if large
600g (1lb 5oz) gooseberries, washed, stems removed and halved if large
80ml (scant ⅓ cup) water
40ml (2½ Tbsp) freshly squeezed lemon juice
800g (4 cups) white granulated sugar

For method: see the jam process on page 112 with notes below, for combining seasonal fruits see page 118, and for set-testing and jarring see page 114.

Notes
- Try to match the flavour profiles of each fruit and use fruits that help each other in pectin amounts for a better set. Suggestions: rhubarb and strawberry; blackberry, raspberry and strawberry; raspberry and orange; blackberry and plum; blackberry and orange; blackberry and peach; plum and lime; apricot and peach; the list is endless.
- When mixing with citrus fruits, use the zest, juice and flesh to flavour a jam and get the right balance for you.

Clementine and whisky marmalade

Makes 4–5 x 250ml (8½fl oz) jars

1.5kg (3lb 4oz) clementines
700ml (3 cups) water
50ml (3½ Tbsp) freshly squeezed
    lemon juice
2 star anise
1.2kg (6 cups) white granulated sugar
80ml (scant ⅓ cup) whisky

For method: see the marmalade process on page 112 with the notes below, for adding alcohol see page 116, and for set-testing and jarring see page 114.

Notes
- If you don't like whisky then try with the same measure of gin, Campari, tequila or, for that lovely smoky effect, mezcal.
- If alcohol isn't your thing, then take out the star anise and pop in a couple of bay leaves at the start of cooking. Or you could chop up some rosemary or lemon thyme and stir through before jarring.

Rainbow marmalade

Makes 6–8 x 250ml (8½fl oz) jars

1.75kg (3lb 14oz) unwaxed mixed
    citrus fruits (oranges, lemons,
    limes, grapefruit, blood oranges,
    tangerines, clementines)
1.3 litres (5½ cups) water
30ml (2 Tbsp) freshly squeezed
    lemon juice
½ vanilla pod, split lengthways and
    seeds scraped (optional)
1.5kg (7½ cups) white granulated
    sugar

For method: see the marmalade process on page 112 with the notes below, and for set-testing and jarring see page 114.

Note
- Use up the citrus you have in your fruit bowl to make this, or anything local you can get your hands on - it's your choice what you use.

Lemon and poppy-seed marmalade

Makes 5–6 x 250ml (8½fl oz) jars

1.5kg (3lb 4oz) unwaxed lemons
1 litre (generous 4 cups) water
1kg (5 cups) white granulated sugar
2 tsp poppy seeds

For method: see the marmalade process on page 112 with the notes below, for adding spices see page 120, and for set-testing and jarring see page 114.

Notes
- Meyer lemons are best with this recipe as they are not as sour and less acidic (they are cross-bred with mandarins). However, unless you live in the USA or Australia, they can be hard to come by. If you can get them, you may want to add less sugar to this recipe.
- If you find this recipe too sour, try adding other citrus fruits using the same technique, such as pink grapefruit, clementines or blood oranges, to sweeten it up some.
- Instead of poppy seeds, add whisky, gin or rum. Or, stir through 1 teaspoon of dried lavender or a cinnamon stick or vanilla pod at the beginning.

Lime and tequila marmalade

Makes 6–7 x 250ml (8½fl oz) jars

1.5kg (3lb 4oz) unwaxed limes
750ml (3¼ cups) water
30ml (2 Tbsp) freshly squeezed
    lemon juice
1kg (5 cups) white granulated sugar
90ml (⅓ cup) tequila

For method: see the marmalade process on page 112 with the notes below, for adding alcohol see page 116, and for set-testing and jarring see page 114.

Notes
- I like to use mezcal or whisky with this recipe as well.
- Always keep jams and marmalades on the highest heats you can, or the largest elements you have, it's important they can reach the high heat they require to get a good set.
- If you are struggling with your marmalades setting, try the preserving sugars available – these don't have added pectin but larger granules to help with setting citrus fruits.

Grape jelly

I have fond memories of eating grapes at my mother's friend's home in New Plymouth. It felt much like a black-and-white Fellini film, driving through a man-made tunnelled driveway to get to his house, walking through to get to the entrance you were enveloped by an overhead terrace of draping grapes. It was the closest I could get to Italy as a child, much like the clichéd Italian restaurants I would see in the movies. Yet here I was, among it all, in a small town in New Zealand. This grape jelly is the most beautiful colour. It conjures thoughts of me plucking those dark, ruby red grapes direct from the vine, wincing at the bitter outer skin, sucking out the sweet innards while spitting out the unwanted pips.

Makes 2–3 x 250ml (8½fl oz) jars

1.25kg (2lb 12oz) seeded red grapes, unripe are best
400ml (1¾ cups) water
50ml (3½ Tbsp) freshly squeezed lemon juice
about 500g (2½ cups) white granulated sugar (see method)

Sterilize your jars and lids (page 212). Place several small saucers in the freezer.

Place the grapes in a large pan with the water and bring to the boil over a medium–high heat. Once the grapes start to soften, gently mash them with a potato masher. Boil and continue to soften for about 10–15 minutes.

With a jelly bag, or a large piece of muslin (cheesecloth) tied up to make a drip bag, strain out the juice from the pulp into a bowl sitting underneath. This will take 4–6 hours (or preferably overnight). Don't be tempted to squeeze the bag, as this can create cloudiness in your jelly.

The next day, measure the grape juice collected in the bowl. Pour it into a large, wide, low-sided pan, add the lemon juice and start to bring to the boil over a high heat.

Measure the sugar: using 500g (2½ cups) for every 600ml (2½ cups) grape juice produced (like-for-like if measuring in cups, or about 83.5g per 100ml).

Add the measured sugar to the boiling grape juice and stir until dissolved. Bring back to the boil and boil for 12–20 minutes, on the highest heat. Once it starts to look syrupy with heavy, aggressive bubbling, start set-testing (page 114). Keep in mind that you are looking for a prominent wrinkle, so keep boiling and testing every 2–3 minutes until you are there.

Jellies can be stored in a cool, dark place for up to 12–18 months. Once opened, store in the fridge and eat within 6–8 weeks.

Notes
- Grapes have medium pectin and acidity levels (page 115), so it's best to use the least ripe grapes you can find to assist the setting. Also, the seeds and skins help with the pectin levels too.
- This recipe makes a jelly which is the consistency of thick honey, so if you want one that has a harder set then use a pectin sugar, such as jam sugar, or a teaspoon of rapid-set pectin powder mixed through your sugar measure.

Rhubarb and hibiscus jammed French toast

I came up with this recipe when I had some stale brioche and was trying to think of an imaginative way to use it up. It was breakfast time, and I had eggs, cream and milk, so it was only a matter of connecting the dots. And, of course, I always want to add a preserving element to my creations.

Serves 2

2 thick-cut slices of brioche bread, about 2–2.5cm (¾in) thick (Homemade, page 198)
4–6 tsp Rhubarb and Hibiscus Jam (page 122), chilled
3 medium free-range eggs
50ml (3½ Tbsp) whole milk
50ml (3½ Tbsp) double (heavy) cream, plus extra to serve
½ tsp vanilla extract
¼ tsp ground cinnamon
2 Tbsp unsalted butter, or more if needed
maple syrup, to serve (optional)

Using a sharp knife, make a deep and wide slit along one of the long sides of the brioche crust, creating a type of pocket. With a butter knife, craftily spread 2–3 teaspoons of the jam inside the bread, as deep inside this pocket as you can. Repeat for the second slice.

In a bowl, whisk together the eggs with the milk, cream, vanilla and cinnamon. Pour into a small, shallow dish, around the size of your bread slices. Soak the jam-filled bread slices in the liquid for at least 5–6 minutes, flipping once so they are thoroughly soaked through.

Melt the butter in a large frying pan over a medium heat. When gently sizzling, add your soaked slices, increase the heat slightly and fry for 2–3 minutes on each side until golden brown and the egg has set a little.

Serve hot from the pan, whole or sliced in half so you can see the jam inside, with jugs of maple syrup and cream to drizzle over.

Notes
- The brioche doesn't have to be stale to make this, but it's a great way to use up thickly sliced stale bread if you have it.
- Get creative and try this recipe with a thick slice of seeded bread.
- Substitute with any jam, jelly or marmalade you desire; even try a nut butter.
- Serve with matching fresh fruit on top, such as blueberries, blackberries or raspberries, with whipped cream instead of the sweetness of maple syrup.

Notes

- Buy a digital thermometer: the temperature is important for thickening your custard and kills off any unwanted, harmful bacteria.
- If your custard has scrambled slightly, just sieve out any lumps.
- Refrigerate your custard overnight if you can. The longer you "age" it before churning, the better the final consistency.
- Follow the ice-cream machine's manufacturer's manual - timings may differ.
- If you don't have an ice-cream machine, freeze the custard, whisking every 45 minutes with a hand whisk. Do this two times, then stir every 30 minutes with a metal spoon until completely frozen.
- You can use any soft-set jam you already have for this recipe, or if you have a harder-set jam simply loosen it with a little water before rippling it through your ice cream.

Rhubarb and hibiscus ripple ice cream

I love ice cream. I'd go so far as to say I have an obsession with it and have managed to befriend many small producers in London (and some elsewhere in the UK). I've had an ice-cream machine for many years but it's only recently that I've perfected the recipe, never quite knowing the true skill it involved. So, with my many fails and now successes, my main advice is: don't over-churn, as it turns buttery. Read my notes opposite too, as these will help your results.

Makes about 800–900ml (27–30fl oz)

300ml (1¼ cups) milk
260ml (1 cup plus 2 Tbsp) double (heavy) cream
pinch of sea salt
½ vanilla pod, split lengthways
4 medium free-range egg yolks (45–50g/1¾–2oz)
110g (generous ½ cup) golden granulated sugar
7–8 Tbsp Rhubarb and Hibiscus Jam (page 122), chilled

In a large saucepan, gently warm the milk, cream and salt with the vanilla seeds scraped from the pod (pop the pod in too) over a medium-low heat until you see it start to steam slightly with small bubbles starting to appear. Stir occasionally with a spatula, removing any lumps in the corners of the pan and any skin that might have formed.

Whisk the egg yolks in a large bowl, then whisk in the sugar. In a steady stream, pour in the warmed milk and cream, whisking as you go until the sugar has dissolved.

Return the mixture to the pan and warm over a medium-low heat, continuing to whisk, until it reaches 82°C (180°F) on a digital thermometer. Remove from the heat and quickly cool the custard down by pouring into a large bowl sitting in a tub of iced water. Whisk quickly to bring it down to room temperature. Cover and refrigerate for at least 4–12 hours. This is called the "aging" stage.

Once aged, slowly churn in an ice-cream machine for 15–25 minutes (according to the manufacturer's instructions). It should be thick in texture, like a soft-serve, and doubled in size. Spoon it into an airtight container, adding the jam as you layer it in, then rippling it through with the handle of a spoon. Snugly cover the top with a piece of baking paper and seal with the lid. Freeze for at least 4 hours.

Remove from the freezer 10 minutes before scooping and serving, for a softer texture.

Pear and cardamom granola crumble with vanilla custard

I'm one of those people who love a Sunday roast in a pub - it's my comfort place. Drinking red wine, slightly hungover from the night before, reading the Sunday papers without talking to the friend who has joined me to feast. Actually, that is one of my pre-requisites, that there is to be very little discourse, a time to contemplate, reflect. Over the years, it has become a pursuit of mine to discover the best the UK has to offer. Crumble most definitely has to be on the menu to complete this silent meal and, luckily, this seems to be a staple on a Sunday. But, sometimes, they're just made better at home.

Serves 6

Crumble topping
90g (¾ cup) plain (all-purpose) flour
40g (scant ½ cup) ground almonds
pinch of sea salt
140g (scant ⅔ cup) unsalted butter, cold, cut into cubes
50g (⅔ cup) rolled (old-fashioned) porridge oats
90g (scant ½ cup) golden or white granulated sugar
90g (⅔ cup) whole almonds, roughly chopped

Base
300ml (1¼ cups) water
50g (¼ cup) golden or white granulated sugar
pared zest and juice of 1 lemon
4 cardamom pods, gently crushed
1 cinnamon stick
I bay leaf
4 firm but ripe pears (Comice, Williams or fat Conference), peeled, cored and cut into halves, wedges or 2cm (¾in) cubes
300–350g (10½–12oz) Pear and Cardamom Jam (page 122)

To serve
600ml (2½ cups) thick vanilla custard or Crème Pâtissière (page 206)

Preheat the oven to 180°C (160°C fan/350°F/gas mark 4).

For the crumble topping, mix together the flour, ground almonds and salt in a large bowl. Using your fingertips, rub in the butter until it starts forming lumps, similar to breadcrumbs, leaving in some of the bigger lumps. Mix through the oats, sugar and chopped almonds and set aside.

For the base, combine the water, sugar, pared lemon zest and juice, cardamom, cinnamon stick and bay leaf in a large saucepan and gently bring to the boil. Place the pears into this syrup (in batches, if necessary), then reduce the heat and cook for 4–5 minutes. Remove the pears, reserving the syrup and set aside.

Spread the jam all over the base of a large, deep baking dish (24 x 18cm/10 x 7in). Place the pears on top and drizzle over 6 tablespoons of the spiced syrup. Sprinkle over the crumble topping.

Bake in the middle of the oven for 20–30 minutes until the crumble topping is golden brown, rotating the dish in the oven to cook evenly if necessary.

Meanwhile, prepare your custard/crème pâtissière.

Remove the crumble from the oven and let rest for 5 minutes before serving with a jug of hot custard.

Notes
- You can easily halve this recipe if you are cooking for just 2 people.
- You can also make this in individual servings by distributing the elements evenly among smaller ramekins.
- Try with other fruits and jams: blackberries with apple jam, apples with apple jam, making sure to stew any harder fruits, like apple, for a little longer in the spiced syrup.
- Or mix and match the fruit-to-jam combo flavours: apples with blackberry jam, rhubarb with strawberry jam.

Pear and cardamom almond cake with sweet vanilla labneh

I frequently make this cake for lunch for the students at my workshops. It's my go-to for showcasing how the jam they made that day can easily be transformed into a cake. This also works seasonally, using different fruits and jam for that particular month: apricot jam with apricots, raspberry jam with raspberries, pear jam with pears. So, it can be adapted for any jam you have in your condiment ghost-town, using the season's fresh fruit and dressed with a few flaked almonds before baking. My students love it and are always asking for the recipe, even though they are there to make preserves, not cake. It's an incredibly easy and delicious cake to whip up if you need a quick go-to in your repertoire.

Serves 8–10

200g (2 cups) ground almonds or almond flour
200g (1½ cups) self-raising (self-rising) flour
200g (1 cup) golden or white granulated sugar
pinch of sea salt
200g (¾ cup plus 2 Tbsp) unsalted butter, cubed and softened, plus extra for greasing
1 tsp vanilla extract
3 medium free-range eggs, at room temperature
150–200g (½–⅔ cup) Pear and Cardamom Jam (page 122)
1 large pear (Conference or Concorde), peeled or not (as you wish), cored and cut into 12 wedges
40–50g (½ cup) flaked (slivered) almonds
Demerara sugar, for sprinkling

To serve
Sweet Labneh with vanilla (page 204), Greek yoghurt or crème fraîche

Preheat the oven to 180°C (160°C fan/350°F/gas mark 4). Grease and line the base and sides of a 23cm (8in) loose-bottomed cake pan with some baking paper.

In a stand mixer or large bowl, mix together the ground almonds, flour, sugar and salt. Add the soft butter, vanilla and one egg at a time, mixing until fully combined. The mixture will be firm, not runny like other cake batters.

Spread half of the cake batter into the prepared cake pan, covering the base as evenly as you can. Spoon dollops of jam on top of this layer, trying not to go too close to the edges. Top with the remaining batter, carefully spreading it over to cover the surface of the jam. Gently push the pear wedges down into the batter in a decorative spiral pattern, then sprinkle over the almond flakes and gently press these down.

Bake in the middle of the oven for 40–50 minutes, or until the top is golden and an inserted skewer comes out clean. Remove from the oven and allow to stand for 10–15 minutes before removing from the pan.

Sprinkle with Demerara sugar and serve with sweet vanilla labneh, yoghurt or crème fraîche.

This cake will keep in a cake tin or sealed airtight container for 3–5 days.

Note
- Alternatives: peaches and peach jam, plums and plum jam, loquats with loquat jam, blackberries with blackberry jam... you get the idea.

Apricot and cacao cobbler with vanilla ice cream

Desserts, for me, need to be clean and not necessarily too sweet. I like tart, sharp and sour tones on my palate - a refreshing way to finish a meal. That's why I've untraditionally chosen apricots instead of peaches for this cobbler, peaches being too sweet a choice for me. The jam creates a slightly sweet element, the ice cream a creaminess, and there is the crunch of nuts and a hot, chewy, biscuity crust but the apricots bring something a bit bitter, something unexpected.

Serves 4–6

600g (1lb 5oz) apricots, stoned (pitted) and each cut into eighths
1 Tbsp lemon juice
250g (scant 1 cup) Apricot and Cacao Nib Jam (page 123)
2 tsp cornflour (cornstarch)
4 tsp warm water

Crust
200g (1½ cups) plain (all-purpose) flour
150g (¾ cup) light or dark brown/ muscovado sugar
1 tsp baking powder
1 tsp ground ginger
¼ tsp sea salt
180g (generous ¾ cup) unsalted butter, cubed, softened, plus extra for greasing

Topping
2 Tbsp golden or white granulated sugar
¾ tsp ground cinnamon
6-7 Tbsp flaked (slivered) almonds, lightly toasted

To serve
sea salt
vanilla ice cream (Homemade without the jam ripple, page 135)

Preheat the oven to 200°C (180°C fan/400°F/gas mark 6).

Combine the apricots with the lemon juice and jam in a saucepan and warm over a medium heat, stirring, for 6-8 minutes. Mix the cornflour with the warm water and slowly pour into the pan, stirring until well combined and slightly thickened.

To make the crust, mix all of the dry ingredients together in a stand mixer or large bowl. Add the soft butter, a little at a time, mixing until it all comes together into a thick, cookie-like dough.

Lightly grease a deep (24 x 18cm/10 x 7in) baking dish with butter and spread the apricot/jam mixture to cover the base. Use a large spoon or ice cream scoop to evenly spoon about 8 scoops of crust dough on top of the apricots, leaving gaps in between (it spreads when baking).

Bake in the middle of the oven for 30 minutes.

Mix together the sugar, cinnamon and almonds for the topping. Remove the cobbler from the oven and sprinkle over the topping, then bake for a further 10-15 minutes until golden brown and the crust has spread out to cover the top.

Remove from the oven and leave to cool for about 10 minutes. Serve each portion with a pinch of sea salt and a large scoop of ice cream to melt in the middle.

Once cooled, this will keep, covered, in the fridge for 4-5 days. Eat cold or warmed up.

Note
- Make alternative cobblers from a variety of fruits and jam: peaches and peach jam, plums and plum jam, loquats with loquat jam or blackberries with blackberry jam - it's not strictly bound to the stone fruits.

Dark chocolate and apricot jam pots with toasted almonds

To showcase how to use jam in other ways, other than on toast, make up these simple and quick choc pots, which always impress. Dark chocolate matches well with apricot, pear, orange and raspberries, so you can use any jam or marmalade you have in the cupboard or fridge. If you're not a fan of dark chocolate, substitute it for milk or even white chocolate. Toppings, too, can vary. Here, I use toasted almond flakes, but try other nuts, ground coffee, coconut flakes, dehydrated berries, fruit slices or candied citrus peel. Create your own combinations.

Makes 6 x 130ml (5fl oz) glasses/ramekins/teacups

230g (¾ cup) Apricot Jam (page 123, made with or without cacao nibs)
180g (6½oz) dark chocolate (at least 70 per cent cocoa solids)
300ml (1¼ cups) double (heavy) cream
2 large free-range egg yolks
2–3 Tbsp flaked (slivered) almonds, lightly toasted

Tahini cream (optional)
200g (1 cup) double (heavy) or whipping cream
1 Tbsp good-quality tahini paste

Spoon 2–3 heaped teaspoons of jam into the bottom of your glasses/ramekins and chill in the fridge.

Roughly break up the chocolate in a large bowl.

Heat the cream in a saucepan over a medium–low heat until it just starts to bubble around the edges and come to a very light simmer. Pour immediately over the chocolate and stir rapidly so that the chocolate melts completely and is smooth in texture. Beat in one egg yolk at a time until thoroughly mixed.

Ladle the mixture equally among the six chilled pots so that they are about three-quarters full. Gently tap the pots on the work surface to level out the chocolate a bit and chill in the fridge for at least 2 hours. They can be made the night before and kept in the fridge for up to 48 hours.

Take the pots out of the fridge 5 minutes before serving, giving you time to gently toast the almond flakes to a golden brown. Once cool, sprinkle a few on top of each choc pot.

Make the tahini cream, if using, by simply whisking the double cream and the tahini together into soft peaks. Serve in a side dish with the choc pots to balance out the richness.

Note
- Alternative suggestions: dark chocolate, raspberry jam, toasted cobnuts; dark chocolate, pear jam, cacao nibs; milk chocolate, marmalade, ground coffee beans; white chocolate, blackberry jam, pistachios; white chocolate, pineapple jam, coconut flakes.

Peach and mint jam hand pies or mini galettes

This recipe is a two-in-one using the same spiced pastry. Both versions are equally easy to achieve, depending on whether you are after a pop tart to hand out at a children's birthday party or if you want to impress at a dinner party with individual mini galettes. Both use the same ingredients dressed in two different ways. I always try to have pre-made pastry in my freezer, so these become super-simple to put together. All you need to do is defrost it to make an impressive dessert for children and adults alike.

Makes 14–16 hand pies or 6 mini galettes

Pastry
210g (1⅔ cups) plain (all-purpose) flour, plus extra for dusting
1 Tbsp golden or white caster (superfine) sugar
½ tsp sea salt
½ tsp ground cinnamon
pinch of grated or ground nutmeg
finely grated zest of ¼ lemon or orange
120g (½ cup) unsalted butter, cold, cubed
140g (⅔ cup) plain Greek-style yoghurt, cold
vegetable or sunflower oil, for greasing
1 medium free-range egg, lightly beaten with 1 tsp water
golden or white granulated sugar, for sprinkling

Filling for hand pies
14–16 Tbsp Peach and Mint Jam (page 123), cold
1 peach, chopped into 1cm (½in) cubes

Filling for mini galettes
12 Tbsp Peach and Mint Jam (page 123), cold
1–2 peaches, chopped into 1cm (½in) cubes or wedges

Make the pastry the day before. Mix together the flour, sugar, salt, spices and zest in a large bowl. Add the cold butter and rub it into the flour with your fingertips until it resembles fine breadcrumbs, without any large butter bits. Add a little more flour if needed. Make a well in the middle, add the yoghurt and bring it together with a fork.

Turn the pastry out onto a lightly floured work surface and knead a couple of times before working it into a ball – it should be a bit tacky and not too firm. Divide into 2 rounds and place in an airtight container or wrap and chill for at least 6–8 hours (or freeze for later and defrost overnight in the fridge).

To make the hand pies
Line a large baking sheet with baking paper and very lightly grease with oil.

Take out one of the pastry rounds and roll out on a lightly dusted work surface, turning, rolling and flipping, to about 3mm (⅛in) thick. With an 11–12cm (4½in) round cookie cutter, cut out circles, gathering and re-rolling the scraps. Repeat with the second pastry round until you have 14–16 discs.

Place 1 tablespoon of jam and 2–4 peach cubes in the middle of each disc, lightly brush one edge with the egg wash, fold the pastry over into a semi-circle and seal. Take a fork and press along the sealed edge, then poke 2 small slits in the top with a sharp knife so the steam can escape. Repeat with the second pastry ball until you have filled all the pies. Place them on the prepared baking sheet 2cm (¾in) apart and chill for at least 30 minutes.

Meanwhile, preheat the oven to 210°C (190°C fan/ 425°F/gas mark 7).

Remove the pies from the fridge, brush with the remaining egg wash and sprinkle over some sugar. Bake in the middle of the oven for 15–20 minutes until golden brown, turning the sheet at least once during baking for an even brown.

To make the mini galettes
Line a large baking sheet with baking paper and very lightly grease with oil.

Take out one of the pastry balls and start to soften by rolling out on a lightly floured work surface, then divide into 3. Roll each third to a 19cm (7½in) diameter circle. Repeat with the remaining pastry to get 6 circles.

Place 2 tablespoons of jam in the middle of each circle, spreading it to about 2–3cm (¾–1in) from the edge, then decoratively arrange your cubes or wedges of peach on top. Fold the edges inwards to enclose the filling, but leaving an inner circle of fruit exposed. Place each galette on the baking sheet, spaced 2cm (¾in) apart, and chill for at least 30 minutes.

Meanwhile, preheat the oven to 210°C (190°C fan/ 425°F/gas mark 7).

Remove from the fridge, brush with the egg wash and sprinkle over some sugar. Bake in the middle of the oven for 15–20 minutes until golden brown, turning the sheet at least once during baking for an even brown.

Notes
- Eat hot or cooled, served with or without cream, whipped or runny.
- Store in an airtight container in the fridge for up to 5 days. They can be warmed in a low oven for 20 minutes.
- Freeze, pre-baked, for up to 1 month. To bake from frozen, add about 8 minutes to the cooking time. Freeze baked and add 8 minutes to the warming time.
- Pair a variety of jams with their matching fruits, or mix it up: rhubarb with strawberry jam, blackberries with peach jam, apricots with fig jam.
- Fill the galettes with a layer of thick custard/crème pâtissière (page 206), then drizzle with jam and top with seasonal fruit.

Peach jam lemon possets

This recipe is a common contender in my workshop classes. When summer appears, the peaches appear, and I love the combination of this zesty, creamy, peachy, light sweetener. It's a summery dessert but isn't solely restricted to the summery flavours. It's versatile according to the season - I've used the same lemon posset on top of blackberry jam, raspberry jam and apricot jam.

Makes 6 x 130ml (5fl oz) glasses/ ramekins/cups/moulds

4–5 Tbsp Peach and Mint Jam (page 123)
zest of 2 lemons, plus 80ml (3½ Tbsp) freshly squeezed lemon juice
500ml (generous 2 cups) double (heavy) cream
100g (½ cup) golden or white caster (superfine) sugar
1 peach, stoned (pitted) and cut into slices (optional)

Spoon 2 heaped teaspoons of jam into the bottom of your glasses/ramekins.

In a medium saucepan, gently heat the cream over a medium-low heat until it starts to slightly steam and small bubbles begin to appear on the surface. Stir in the sugar until dissolved, ensuring it doesn't stick to the crease in the pan. Increase the heat a little and slowly bring to a gentle simmer for about 1 minute. Turn off the heat and stir through the lemon zest and juice and then rest for 1–2 minutes.

Pour the warm liquid posset evenly among each glass/ramekin, carefully, on top of the jam.

Cool to room temperature, cover and chill in the fridge for 4–6 hours until the acid in the citrus reacts with the fats in the cream and sets.

Serve straight from the fridge with an optional slice of peach on top.

Note
- Other jams also work well with lemon possets. Blackberries pair particularly well with lemon, so try a blackberry jam with a big plump blackberry dusted in icing (confectioners') sugar on top.
- To serve, you could try candied mint, basil or petals, such as rose or lilac.
- Try something crunchy on top, like toasted hazelnuts or leftover crumble mix (page 136). Or be more daring and try them with toasted salted sourdough crumbs.

Raspberry jam and peanut butter brownies

Everyone loves a brownie, right? Make this recipe to use up the end of that raspberry jam you have in the fridge, or try it with my recipe for Raspberry and Elderflower Jam (page 124). Raspberries are the perfect match for dark chocolate, and the jam makes a playfully reminiscent match with the peanut butter. It's where childhood meets adulthood.

Makes 15

250g (1 cup plus 2 Tbsp) unsalted butter, plus extra for greasing
250g (9oz) dark chocolate (at least 70 per cent cocoa solids)
100g (1 cup) cocoa powder
6 large free-range eggs
350g (1¾ cups) golden caster (superfine) sugar
100g (¾ cup) plain (all-purpose) flour
80g (generous ¾ cup) ground almonds
100g (½ cup) crunchy peanut butter
100-150g (⅓-scant ½ cup) Raspberry and Elderflower Jam (page 124)

Preheat the oven to 200°C (180°C fan/400°F/gas mark 6). Line and grease a deep 20 x 30cm (8 x 12in) baking pan with baking paper.

Roughly chop the butter and dark chocolate and melt in a bowl set over a pan of simmering water (ensure the bottom of the bowl does not touch the water), stirring occasionally until completely melted. Remove from the heat and whisk through the cocoa powder, then set aside to cool.

In a large bowl, whisk together the eggs and sugar until pale and creamy. Gently fold through the melted chocolate mix until smooth, then sift in the flour and gently fold through with the ground almonds until well combined.

Pour the batter into the baking pan, spreading it to the edges. Spoon in dots of peanut butter and jam, then roughly swirl them into the batter with a spatula.

Bake in the middle of the oven for 20–30 minutes, or until the top has a slight crust and a gentle wobble in the middle (cooking time may vary according to your oven, so check at 20 minutes and then every 5 minutes).

Remove from the oven and leave to cool completely so it firms up before removing from the pan. Slice into 15 portions.

Notes
- Substitute the jam for any other you have that you like to match with dark chocolate, like apricot, blackberry or gooseberry.
- If you don't fancy the saltiness of peanut butter, just omit it and double up on the jam. Have fun with this and add fresh fruits/berries as well.
- Try using white chocolate to make a raspberry and peanut butter blondie - simply substitute the dark chocolate and cocoa powder with 300g (10½oz) white chocolate and add 20g (¾oz) extra ground almonds.

Victoria sponge with raspberry and elderflower jam and cream

My close friend Taj, who introduced me to my husband, is an amazing baker. She owned tearooms in Brighton and now resides in Ligné, the Cognac region of France. Here, she caters for weddings and hen parties, for those eloping to the most romantic setting in the world. I go to her for all the classics as she is incredibly talented. This recipe is under her guidance for a fail-proof Victoria sponge layer cake.

Serves 8–10

230g (1 cup) unsalted butter, softened, cubed, plus extra for greasing
190g (scant 1 cup) caster (superfine) sugar
4 medium free-range eggs, at room temperature
¾ tsp vanilla extract or paste
230g (1¾ cups) self-raising (self-rising) flour, or plain with 3 level tsp baking powder
pinch of sea salt
1½ tsp baking powder
50–100ml (3½–7 Tbsp) milk, if needed
150g (½ cup) Raspberry and Elderflower Jam (page 124), loosened with 1 Tbsp boiling water if needed
200ml (scant 1 cup) lightly whipped cream or mascarpone
1 Tbsp icing (confectioners') sugar, for dusting (optional)
edible flowers or fresh fruit, to decorate

Preheat the oven to 170°C (150°C fan/325°F/gas mark 3). Grease the bottom and sides of two 19cm (7½in) round cake pans. Line the bottoms with greased circles of baking paper and make one extra circle and grease.

In a stand mixer fitted with the paddle attachment, or a large bowl with an electric hand whisk, cream the butter with the sugar until very pale and fluffy.

In a separate bowl, whisk the eggs with the vanilla. Mix together the flour, salt and baking powder in another bowl.

Add the egg mixture to the creamed butter a little at a time, fully incorporating each time and trying not to overbeat, then fold in the flour mixture, one spoonful at a time, until just combined and the mixture looks smooth. It should drop off your spoon easily when tapped. If it's too stiff, add a little milk and gently fold through to achieve this.

Divide the batter equally between the prepared pans and level out with a spatula, making a dip in the middle of each. Place the extra greased paper disc on the top of one of the cakes for an even rise. Bake in the middle of the oven for 15–18 minutes or until an inserted skewer comes out clean. You can bake these in batches, for less time, if you only have one cake pan or no room in your oven for two. Leave to cool in the pans for 10 minutes before turning out on a wire rack to cool completely.

Drizzle the jam over the flat-topped sponge and dress with a thick layer of the whipped cream (or vice versa) and carefully top with the second sponge layer. Dust with icing sugar and decorate with your choice of edible flowers, such as elderflower, rose petals or lavender, or with fresh fruit like raspberries or strawberries.

Notes
- You can store the sponge layers in an airtight container for 1-2 days before decorating.
- Substitute the jam for any other you have - I've used apricot, rhubarb and gooseberry jams as alternatives.

Fig and Cointreau Dutch baby pancakes with hazelnuts and citrus cream

Figs always feel exotic to me. My husband's uncle and auntie's summer home is in Ostuni, Puglia, where figs grow wild. I say home as they live there for a quarter of the year and have done for almost 20 years. We visit them often in the summer months where the figs grow amid their olive grove and it's a pure joy to pick them, plump and sweet, directly from the trees. A million miles away, what better way to indulge than with a breakfast of Dutch baby pancakes and fig and Cointreau jam.

Serves 2–4

3 large free-range eggs
85g (scant ⅔ cup) plain (all-purpose) flour
¼ tsp baking powder
¼ tsp ground cinnamon
120ml (½ cup) milk (whole, oat or almond)
1 Tbsp golden or white caster (superfine) sugar
¼ tsp sea salt
½ tsp vanilla extract
20g (1½ Tbsp) unsalted butter

Toppings
180–200g (⅔ cup) Fig and Cointreau Jam (page 124)
15–20g (2–2½ Tbsp) hazelnuts, roughly chopped, lightly toasted with a small pinch of salt
zest of ½ orange
150ml (⅔ cup) double (heavy) cream
icing (confectioners') sugar, for dusting (optional)

In a large bowl, vigorously whisk the eggs for about 2 minutes until light and fluffy. Sift in the flour, baking powder and cinnamon and whisk in until just combined.

Mix the milk, sugar, salt and vanilla in a jug and pour into the batter in a slow, steady stream, continuously whisking until the batter is smooth with no lumps. Rest the batter at room temperature for at least 1 hour.

Preheat the oven to 240°C (220°C fan/475°F/gas mark 9). Place two 15cm (6in) cast-iron skillets or ovenproof frying pans in the middle of the oven for at least 10 minutes.

Use oven gloves to remove one skillet at a time, closing the oven door immediately. Quickly swirl in half of the butter before pouring in half of the batter, swirling it around so it coats the bottom and sides of the pan. Place back in the oven, then repeat with the second skillet. Bake for 13–15 minutes without opening the oven door, until puffed up and golden brown.

Serve hot from the oven, with the handles of the skillets safely wrapped with a cloth, topped with dollops of jam, toasted hazelnuts, orange zest and cream drizzled over. Dust with icing sugar if you wish.

Notes
- You can also make one large Dutch baby pancake in a 25cm (10in) skillet or ovenproof frying pan. Cast iron works best as it conducts the heat.
- Use alternative jams, such as blueberry, blackberry or cherry, and top with fresh berries and cream.
- Try other toasted nuts to add texture and a bit of crunch.

Fig and Cointreau jammy Newtons

I wish I had a baked slice named after me, but unfortunately this is named after the Massachusetts town Newton. Fig Newtons were recommended in the late nineteenth century as a solution to certain ailments and to aid digestion. They are half-cake, half-biscuit with a fig jam filling. My adaption is a touch of citrus to complement the fig and a little Cointreau. Don't stop at figs – these can be filled with a variety of firmer-set jams: try mixed berry, apple, strawberry or raspberry.

Makes 18–20

140g (scant ⅔ cup) unsalted butter,
    at room temperature, diced,
    plus extra for greasing
100g (½ cup) light brown sugar
1 medium free-range egg plus
    2 medium free-range egg yolks,
    at room temperature
1 tsp vanilla paste/extract
2 Tbsp runny honey
1 Tbsp orange juice
170g (1¼ cups) wholemeal flour
250g (scant 2 cups) plain
    (all-purpose) white flour,
    plus extra for dusting
pinch of ground cloves
¾ tsp ground ginger
½ tsp ground cinnamon
¼ tsp sea salt
½ tsp orange zest
300–350g (10½–12oz) Fig and
    Cointreau Jam (page 124)
1 egg, lightly beaten, for egg wash

Make the dough in advance as it needs time to chill. In a stand mixer fitted with the paddle attachment, or a large bowl with an electric whisk, cream the butter and sugar together on a medium speed until very pale and fluffy. Add the egg and the egg yolks, one at a time, completely combining before adding the next. Mix through the vanilla, honey and orange juice.

Mix the flours, spices, salt and zest in a separate bowl, then fold through the butter mixture, a spoonful at a time, until combined. Bring it together in your hands, then divide into equal thirds. Roll and flatten each third slightly into rectangles and place in airtight containers. Chill for at least 3 hours.

Fill a piping bag with the jam and keep chilled. Line and lightly grease a large baking sheet.

Take a portion of dough and roll between 2 layers of baking paper into as even a rectangle as possible, 11 x 35cm (4½ x 14in) and 3–4mm (⅛–⅙in) thick. Cut bits off and mould them back in, if necessary, to make neat corners. If it starts to get too soft and tacky, you may need to chill again to firm up the butter.

With the longest edge of the dough facing you, pipe a very thick (2cm/¾in) tube of cold jam down the middle along its length. Use the paper to lift from the back and fold the dough over on itself, just over the line of jam. Continue rolling so it overlaps into a gentle spiral. Press down, flattening the length's edge and sealing into a tubular teardrop shape. Place on the baking sheet and chill in the fridge. Repeat with the other dough portions to make 3 rolls. Trim off the ends and freeze for 30 minutes.

(continues)

Fig and Cointreau jammy Newtons *continued*

Preheat the oven to 190°C (170°C fan/375°F/gas mark 5).

Egg wash the top of the Newtons and bake in the middle of the oven for 12–15 minutes or until slightly puffy and golden brown. Remove from the oven and immediately trim off the edges then cut into 4.5cm (1¾in) pieces. Place in an airtight container while they are still warm, to get the cakey, softer texture of a Fig Newton. They will keep in the container for up to 3 weeks.

Notes
- Try a variety of jam alternatives, such as apricot or blackberry jam.
- Add nuts for texture, such as almonds or hazelnuts.

Jam-filled wholemeal hamantaschen

Hamantaschen ("ears of Haman") cookies are traditionally eaten on the Jewish holiday of Purim. This triangular-shaped cookie is meant to represent the ears of the villain Haman or his three-cornered hat. According to the Book of Esther, Queen Esther, a Jew married to the Persian King Ahasuerus, is the reason the Jews were saved from Haman's slaughter in the city of Shushan in the 1500s. This recipe is in homage to my friend Felicity Spector, who first introduced me to these wonderful morsels.

Makes 24–26

100g (scant ½ cup) unsalted butter, at room temperature
80g (generous ⅓ cup) golden or white granulated sugar
1 medium egg, at room temperature
½ tsp vanilla paste/extract
¾ tsp lemon zest
230g (1¾ cups) light wholemeal or light spelt flour
pinch of sea salt
2–4 tsp water
plain (all-purpose) flour, for dusting
150g (½ cup) hard-set jam, Blackberry and Hazelnut works well (page 125)
milk, for brushing

Make the dough in advance as it needs time to chill. In a stand mixer fitted with the paddle attachment, or an electric whisk, cream the butter and sugar together until pale and fluffy. Mix in the egg, vanilla and lemon zest until completely combined.

Sift the flour and salt together in a separate bowl, then mix one large spoon at a time into the butter mix. It should start to lump together into a crumbly texture. Use your hands to knead without overworking, adding teaspoonfuls of water at a time, but only enough to bring the dough together so it's smoother and tacky to the touch. Divide the dough in half, mould each into a ball and place in an airtight container. Chill for at least 4–8 hours or freeze and defrost in the fridge for 10–14 hours.

Preheat the oven to 200°C (180°C fan/400°F/gas mark 6), line a baking sheet with baking paper and lightly dust a work surface with flour.

Take one of the dough balls and roll it out to 3–4mm (⅛–⅛in) thick, turning, flipping and dusting as you roll. Cut out as many circles as you can with a 7.5cm (3in) round cookie cutter and place them on a plate covered with a damp dish towel. Gather and re-roll the scraps and repeat. Depending on how many cookies you would like to make, you can repeat this with the second dough ball.

Working with one circle of dough at a time, place a teaspoonful of jam in the middle and gently fold in the rounded edges in a 3-part fold to form a triangle leaving an exposed inner triangle of jam. Gently pinch each overlap to seal the folds. Place on the lined baking sheet and repeat. Chill the cookies for 20–30 minutes before baking.

Brush with milk and bake in the middle of the oven for 15–20 minutes. Eat warm or cool on a wire rack. They will keep for 6–7 days in an airtight container.

Note

- I love this with blackberry and hazelnut jam, where a little nut flavour comes through, but try this with any hard-set jams or marmalades. The runnier, soft-set ones won't sit as upright and can run out when baking. Use this recipe as a means for using up all the odds and ends of the jams in your fridge, making a colourful palette of rainbow cookies.

Ginger-crust cheesecake with blackberry and hazelnut jam

I'm one of those rare people who can't do hazelnut and chocolate - I just don't think they are an ideal match. I prefer hazelnuts with creamier flavours, like yoghurt, ice cream, burrata or a cheesecake.

You can definitely use any fridge-foraged jam to top the crust base of this baked cheesecake, but try one that is rich and decadent in flavour, like plum, prune or damson, then sprinkle a few crushed hazelnuts on top. If you want to try it with my Blackberry and Hazelnut Jam, refer to page 125 and make your own.

Serves 8–10

Crust
100g (scant ½ cup) unsalted butter, plus extra for greasing
115g (4oz) ginger nut biscuits
115g (4oz) digestive biscuits (Graham crackers)
pinch of sea salt
1 tsp ground ginger

Cheesecake filling
520g (2⅓ cups) cream cheese, at room temperature
300g (scant 1½ cups) soured cream or mascarpone, at room temperature
140g (scant ¾ cup) caster (superfine) sugar
5 medium free-range eggs, whisked
¾ tsp vanilla extract
finely grated zest of 1 lemon plus 45ml (3 Tbsp) lemon juice
200g (⅔ cup) Blackberry and Hazelnut Jam (page 125), loosened with 1–2 tsp water if needed

Preheat the oven to 180°C (160°C fan/350°F/gas mark 4).

Grease the base and sides of a 20cm (8in) diameter, 7cm (3in) deep, loose-bottomed cake pan and line the sides only with a greased baking paper ring that sits at least 12cm (5in) tall, coming up over the top of the cake pan.

Melt the butter in a small pan. Blitz up the biscuits in a food processor with the salt and ground ginger until it's like breadcrumbs (this also can be achieved by putting the biscuits in a bag and bashing with a rolling pin). Transfer to a bowl and slowly pour the melted butter over the crumbs, mixing as you go until they are completely saturated and darker in appearance.

Firmly pack the crumb into the base of the prepared pan and bake in the middle of the oven for about 14 minutes, turning as it bakes for even golden browning. Set aside to cool and reduce the oven temperature to 160°C (140°C fan/325°F/gas mark 3).

Using a stand mixer or electric whisk, beat the cream cheese with the soured cream until light and fluffy. Mix in the sugar, a little at a time, then fold through the eggs, vanilla, lemon zest and juice.

When the base has cooled, waterproof the cake pan by wrapping up the bottom and sides securely with foil and boil the kettle. Spread a thick layer of jam over the crumb base, then put the cake pan into a deep roasting pan. Fill the roasting pan with the boiling water so that it comes halfway up the sides of the cake pan. Gently pour the cheesecake filling into the

(continues)

Ginger-crust cheesecake *continued*

cake pan until quite close to the top edge of the pan (the baking paper ring will protect it from overflowing). Very carefully transfer to the rack in the middle of the oven. Bake for 80–90 minutes until the filling is slightly puffy, with a gently wobble in the middle and a slight golden tinge on the surface.

Carefully remove the cake from the water bath while still hot, remove the foil and leave to cool in the pan on a rack for at least 2 hours before chilling in the fridge for 8–12 hours. You will notice the cake will shrink as it cools – this is normal.

When removing from the cake pan, use a warmed palette knife to gently ease off the base of the pan. Slice and serve cold. It will keep in the fridge for up to 7 days.

Notes
- If using a 23cm (9in) pan, your cake will turn out shallower with a thinner crumb base.
- Use any thicker, hard-set jam for this cheesecake – try raspberry or blueberry. Or if you prefer a soft jam, like rhubarb or apricot, then drizzle it over the top instead of over the crumb base.

Jam-filled doughnuts

When I want the taste of jam, I never turn to toast. I might have it on granola for breakfast, but I much prefer adding it to my baking, ice cream and, my all-time favourite, doughnuts. There's been a lot of hype in London over doughnuts in the past 8–10 years, ever since the very talented baker Justin Gellatly galvanized these delights while working at St. John Bakery, making them legendary across the land (and sea). Before Justin, when I was a wee girl, this was often a weekend treat when staying with my dad. Eyes wide open, my sisters and I would enter the bakery. Our choice, what would it be? Custard square? Apple turnover? No, for me, a sugar-coated, jam-filled doughnut.

Makes about 8

280g (2 cups) strong bread flour, plus extra for dusting
25g (2 Tbsp) caster (superfine) sugar, plus extra for dusting
½ tsp sea salt
½ tsp baking powder
1 large free-range egg, at room temperature
180ml (¾ cup) lukewarm whole milk, 30–40°C (86–104°F)
7g (1 sachet/2 tsp) fast-action dried yeast
20g (1½ Tbsp) unsalted butter, cubed and softened
olive oil, for greasing
vegetable, sunflower or rapeseed (canola) oil, for deep-frying
260–280g (about 1 cup) jam of your choice, soft-set or loosened hard-set (see note overleaf)

In a stand mixer fitted with the paddle attachment, or in a large bowl, mix together the flour, sugar, salt and baking powder.

In a small bowl, lightly whisk the egg together with the warmed milk.

Add the yeast to the dry ingredients and begin to mix on a slow speed, pouring in the eggy milk in a single stream. Mix until combined, then change to the hook attachment and knead on medium-high speed for 5–6 minutes, or until it starts to cling to the hook in a ball and come away from the sides of the bowl. Use a bread scraper or spatula to occasionally bring it all together, if needed. If mixing by hand, once the ingredients are well combined, remove to a lightly dusted work surface and knead for 10–15 minutes.

Add the softened butter and continue to knead for a further 5–6 minutes until the dough is smooth and shiny in appearance (or a further 8–10 minutes if by hand).

Lightly grease a large bowl with olive oil, form the dough into a ball and place in the bowl. Cover with a damp dish towel and leave to prove at room temperature for 40 minutes–2 hours until doubled in size. This time can vary depending on the temperature of the room (1 hour at 20–22°C (68–72°F) should suffice).

Cut the proved dough into 8 equal parts (each about 65g/2¼oz). Cover with a damp dish towel while you work each into a ball. On a clean work surface, roll the dough pieces by folding the corners into the middle, then flip over and with a cupped hand over the dough, quickly but gently move your hand in a circular motion, barely touching the dough while it rolls under

(continues)

Jam-filled doughnuts *continued*

your hand, rolling it into a perfect ball. Only very lightly dust your surface with flour and only if your dough is too sticky – you will find extra flour doesn't help, as you need the slight friction for the dough to grip and roll.

Lightly grease a large tray with olive oil. Place the balls on the tray (noting the order as this will be the order you fry them) and leaving a 6–7cm (2½–3in) gap between each ball. Cover with lightly oil-greased clingfilm (plastic wrap). Prove for a further 15–20 minutes at room temperature until doubled in size.

Fill a deep-fryer or a deep heavy-based saucepan with enough oil for deep-frying (no more than half-full if using a saucepan). Heat the oil to 170°C (338°F) or until a cube of bread dropped in browns in 40 seconds. Take care, as hot oil can be very dangerous if left unattended.

Deep fry one or two doughnuts at a time, in the order they went on the tray. Place the tray in the fridge between frying so they don't over-prove and make sure the oil comes back to temperature before cooking a new batch. Fry for 2–2½ minutes on each side, or until they turn golden brown. Remove with a large slotted spoon to drain and cool on paper towels, standing them upright to allow the oil to drain off.

Dust the cooled doughnuts with sugar, then use a chopstick to poke a deep hole into the side of each doughnut at the central seam. Fill a piping bag with a 2cm (¾in) hole cut off at the tip (or fitted with a small nozzle), with the soft jam. Push the piping tip deep into the doughnut's hole and squeeze in a generous blob of jam (about 30–35g/1–1¼oz). If you don't have a piping bag, use a clean plastic bag with a corner cut off to pipe the jam in.

Undusted and unfilled, the doughnuts should keep for 1–2 days in an airtight container. Once sugar coated and filled, ideally eat them within 4–6 hours.

Notes
- Use any jam you have. If your jam is a harder set, loosen it by warming it slightly with a little water.
- These are also great filled with different flavoured curds or thick custard (page 206).
- Try dusting with floral or spiced sugars, such as lilac, rose, lavender or cinnamon, cardamom or citrus zest.

Strawberry and gooseberry jammy Eton mess

"Quintessentially English" as they say, this is a dessert that's become more than just about a game of cricket. Originating from Eton College's annual cricket match against the pupils of Harrow School since 1893, this recipe has become an English classic. It is built around strawberries, the fruit that, for me, encapsulates British summers. When the strawberries begin to arrive, the days are starting to get warmer and longer, a new season is on its way, hope is in the air and it's time to bring out the Pimm's.

Makes 4 x 150ml (5fl oz) dessert glasses/bowls

250–300g (9–10½oz) fresh strawberries, hulled, left whole or cut into halves or quarters
2 tsp icing (confectioners') sugar
3 Tbsp Strawberry and Gooseberry Jam (page 125)
2 Tbsp Pimm's or grenadine (optional)
200ml (generous ¾ cup) double (heavy) cream or 150ml (⅔ cup) full-fat coconut milk
¼ tsp vanilla bean paste or extract
freeze-dried or dehydrated strawberries (Homemade, page 210) (optional)

Meringue shards
1 medium egg white or 200ml (generous ¾ cup) aquafaba
50g (¼ cup) caster (superfine) sugar
1½ tsp lemon juice

Make the meringue shards the day before or in the morning. Preheat the oven to 140°C (120°C fan/ 275°F/gas mark 1). Line a large baking sheet with baking paper.

Beat the egg white (or aquafaba) with an electric whisk, adding 1 tablespoon of sugar at a time, to glossy, firm peaks, about 2–4 minutes on a high speed. Ensure the sugar is completely dissolved. Fold through the lemon juice, gently incorporating it without losing too much air. Spread the mixture over the entire baking sheet, as thinly as you can. Bake in the middle of the oven for 15 minutes, then turn the oven off and leave the meringue to cool in the oven for at least 3–4 hours. Remove and break into shards and store in an airtight container.

Place the fresh strawberries in a bowl, sprinkle with the icing sugar and leave to macerate for 20–30 minutes.

Make a syrup in a small pan by warming the jam with the alcohol of your choice.

Whip the cream or coconut milk with the vanilla until light and fluffy.

Assemble in individual stemmed dessert glasses or one large glass bowl to see the layers. Start with a layer of strawberries at the bottom, then add a drizzle of jam syrup and top with a few meringue shards and some of the whipped cream. Repeat these layers until you reach the top, ending with a layer of whipped cream.

Crush or blitz freeze-dried/dehydrated strawberries in a food processor as fine as you wish to make a crumb or dust to sprinkle on top.

Note
- Although Eton mess is traditionally made with strawberries, there's no harm in mixing it up with other fruits and berries. Try fresh blackberries with blackberry jam and vermouth, fresh plums with plum jam and bourbon, fresh peaches with peach jam and rum. Try shaving white, milk or dark chocolate on top.

Mark's marmalade Christmas ham

I live across the world from my family, so I've formed a new family in the UK. My Christmas traditions have changed; however, my mother-in-law is a dream and has adopted some of my Mum's traditions, just so I get a little taste of home at the festive season. My husband joins in by making a marmalade ham for the ham, cheese and tomato grilled croissants my Mum would make every Christmas morning, when we would drink Buck's Fizz (yes, not the rebranded Mimosa) and sit around on the floor to open all our gifts.

Use any marmalade - we just love ours with Clementine and Whisky (page 128); clementines encapsulate the idea of Christmas in the UK for me.

Makes about 750g (1lb 6oz) cooked ham

1–1.2kg (2lb 4oz–2lb 12oz) boneless, unsmoked tied gammon joint
250–300ml (1–1⅓ cups) apple cider
2 Tbsp Clementine and Whisky Marmalade (page 128)
1 tsp honey
1 Tbsp Dijon mustard
2 tsp orange juice or water
6–8 cloves (optional)

Preheat the oven to 200°C (180°C fan/400°F/gas mark 6).

Rinse the gammon in cold water. Pour the cider into a roasting pan, then top up with boiling water to a depth of about 3cm (1in). Place the gammon on a rack that sits above the surface of the liquid, making sure the liquid isn't touching the meat. Wrap a large piece of foil loosely over the meat like a tent, ensuring there is an airtight seal around the edges of the pan but that it doesn't touch the meat (creating a sort of steam balloon around the gammon).

Bake in the middle of the oven for 50–55 minutes per 1kg (2lb 4oz) of meat. Remove from the oven, remove the foil and rest until cool enough to handle. Snip off the string and use a very sharp knife to slice off the tougher skin without removing any of the fat. Score a criss-cross pattern into the fat at 2cm (¾in) intervals.

In a small bowl, mix together the marmalade, honey, mustard and orange juice and generously cover the scored fat with the mixture. Push the cloves, if using, into the scored fat in an intermittent fashion.

Return the gammon to the oven and bake uncovered for a further 25 minutes or until the glaze is golden.

Rest the meat for at least 1 hour before slicing. You can make this a few days ahead of Christmas to lighten the cooking prep on the day – it will keep in the fridge for up to 1–2 weeks.

Note
- Try with any marmalade or jelly you might have in your condiment ghost-town: orange, lime, grapefruit, lemon marmalades; or grape, quince, apple, or medlar jellies.

Marmalade ham, cheese and rocket baguette

Having a sandwich recipe in a cookery book seems a little insulting, I know. We all know how to make a sandwich, right? But sometimes it's easy to get stuck in a pattern with food and I just want to introduce you to marmalade in a baguette. It's different and maybe something you hadn't thought of before and it's also a great everyday way of using up that marmalade you keep getting every year at Christmas.

Serves 2–3

1 French-style baguette
1–1½ Tbsp unsalted butter, at room temperature
1–2 tsp Dijon or multigrain mustard
2 tsp marmalade, any type
3–4 slices of Marmalade Christmas Ham (page 169)
4–5 slices of Brie, Emmental or Cheddar
handful of rocket (arugula)
sea salt and freshly ground black pepper, to taste

Slice the baguette down the middle lengthways, leaving one edge still attached so you can open it like a hinge. Butter the top and bottom of the soft bread inside, then spread mustard on the top half and marmalade on the bottom half. Fold the ham and push in, then top with the cheese and rocket. Season and close the sandwich, gently squeezing it together as you slice it in half.

Half for you, half for a friend.

Note
- Substitute the marmalade for a fruit jelly, quince or medlar, or even a jam
  with bitter notes, such as blackberry or damson.

Steak, mushroom and marmalade pie

This is a pie for Sunday supper, a recipe for a day when you have time to cook, to put the enjoyment back into cooking after a busy week. The beef cooks slowly, absorbing the liquor as it thickens, allowing the flavours to enhance, the marmalade adding a bitter-sweet complexity to the dish. It becomes soft and melt in the mouth.

We don't eat a lot of meat at home. When we do, we make sure we source it sustainably reared from a local butcher - this way, we are not only supporting local businesses but directly benefitting the farmers as well. It doesn't have to be the most expensive cut to make a rich heart-warming meal. Ask your butcher for braising/stewing beef or ready-cubed shin or rump.

Serves 4

Filling
2 Tbsp light olive oil
600g (1lb 5oz) cubed beef, trimmed of some fat, at room temperature
700ml (3 cups) beef or vegetable stock (broth)
2 large red onions, chopped into chunks
1 large garlic clove, finely chopped
170g (6oz) carrots, finely diced
1 celery stalk, finely diced
3 Tbsp plain (all-purpose) flour
3 Tbsp Lime and Tequila Marmalade (page 129)
2 sprigs of thyme
2 dried bay leaves
230g (8oz) chestnut (cremini) mushrooms, chopped into chunks
sea salt and freshly ground black pepper

Pastry crust
50g (3½ Tbsp) unsalted butter, at room temperature, cubed
140g (generous 1 cup) wholemeal or plain white (all-purpose) flour, plus extra for dusting
pinch of sea salt
1 Tbsp coarsely ground black pepper
2 medium egg yolks
3–5 Tbsp water
1 egg, lightly whisked, for egg wash

In a shallow, lidded, heat-safe casserole dish (Dutch oven) or cast-iron pan, about 23cm (9in) in diameter, heat half of the oil over a medium-high heat and brown the beef cubes in 3–4 batches for 1–2 minutes on each side. Remove and set each batch aside in a bowl together.

In a small saucepan, bring the stock to a simmer.

Add the remaining oil to the casserole dish or cast-iron pan and reduce the heat slightly. Add the onions and generously season, then sauté for 5–6 minutes until translucent and glossy. Add the garlic and cook for a further 5–6 minutes. Add the carrots and celery and a ladleful of hot stock, then increase the heat and cook off the stock for 1–2 minutes. Add the browned meat with any of the juices from the bowl, sprinkle over the flour and stir it through, coating the meat and vegetables. Add the remaining stock and stir through the marmalade, thyme and bay leaves. Bring back to the boil, then reduce the heat and cover with a lid. Leave to stew for 1½ hours, stirring intermittently, then remove the lid, pick out the bay leaves and thyme and add the mushrooms. Simmer for a further 30 minutes, occasionally stirring, allowing it to thicken while you make your crust.

For the pastry crust, rub the butter into the flour and salt with your fingers until it resembles fine breadcrumbs. Liberally grind in the pepper, mix in the egg yolks and add enough water so that it starts to come together into a soft rollable dough. Roll into a ball, cover and refrigerate for 20 minutes.

Meanwhile, preheat the oven to 200°C (180°C fan/ 400°F/gas mark 6).

(continues)

Steak and marmalade pie *continued*

Turn off the heat under the stew and let it rest for 5–10 minutes.

On a lightly dusted work surface, roll out the dough to a circle a little wider than the casserole dish/pan and about 3mm (⅛in) thick. Rustically place it on top of the stew, slice 2 slits in the middle for the steam to release, and lightly brush the top with the egg wash. Bake in the middle of the oven for 30–35 minutes, until the crust has hardened and browned.

Serve the pie with your favourite type of creamy mashed potato with mustard, horseradish, parsley, crème fraîche, mascarpone or chopped capers, along with seasonal braised buttery bitter greens, such as cavolo nero, chard, Savoy or hispi cabbage.

Notes
- I like this best with a lime marmalade, but you can substitute the marmalade for any other citrus jam you may have in your condiment ghost-town.
- Make this a vegetarian pie by soaking 500g (2¾ cups) aduki beans, mung beans or red kidney beans. Drain and add to the vegetables when you add the vegetable stock and simmer for 1½ hours. In the last 20-30 minutes of thickening without a lid, stir through 200g (7oz) cubed tofu. Then make the crust and bake in the same way.

Grape-glazed duck with crushed butter beans and creamy spring greens

Glazing with homemade fruit jellies or marmalades is a fun way to incorporate your preserving into your cooking, even when it's not a cake or bread. Try glazing salmon, trout, ham, pork ribs, chicken or wild game with your favourite Seville orange marmalade or that homemade medlar jelly that you never know what to serve with. Although cooking duck may make you feel challenged, this is a surprisingly easy-to-follow recipe. It's quick and tasty and you can whip it up in 30-40 minutes.

Serves 2

Duck
2 free-range duck breasts (about 370g/13oz), trimmed of excess fat
2 tsp light olive oil
2 Tbsp Grape Jelly (page 130)
sea salt, to taste

Greens
40g (3 Tbsp) unsalted butter
2 small garlic cloves, finely chopped
200g (7oz) spring greens, or pointed or Savoy cabbage, cut into 2-3cm (¾-1in) strips
50ml (3½ Tbsp) vegetable stock (broth)
60g (½ cup) peas, fresh or frozen
1 Tbsp crème fraîche
sea salt and freshly ground black pepper, to taste

Butter beans
40g (3 Tbsp) unsalted butter
300g (1½ cups) butter (lima) beans (canned, jarred, or soaked and cooked)
3 Tbsp butter-bean brine from the can/jar or cooking liquor
zest and juice of ½ lemon
sea salt and freshly ground black pepper, to taste

With a very sharp knife, score the skin of the duck in a criss-cross pattern, about 1.5cm (¾in) wide. Salt each side and allow to stand at room temperature for 20–30 minutes.

Pat the duck dry with paper towels. Pour the oil into a cast-iron or large frying pan and place the duck breasts, skin-side down, into the cold pan, rubbing them into the oil. Turn the heat to medium-high. When they start to puff up, press down on each breast for 30–40 seconds. Cook for a further 6–8 minutes, depending on the size of the breasts, then flip and lightly salt the skin. Cook for a further 4–6 minutes (size dependent), until not too rare but not overcooked and tough. "Kiss cook" the fatter-edged side by leaning both breasts up against each other, cooking for a further minute. Remove from the pan and let rest for 5–6 minutes, spooning out 3 tablespoons of the duck fat into a small saucepan.

For the greens, melt the butter in a frying pan over a medium-low heat. Add the garlic and a pinch of salt and gently cook for 1–2 minutes. Stir through the cabbage and season generously. Increase the heat to medium, pour in the stock, cover and cook for 2 minutes. Reduce the heat and add the peas, cover again, and cook for a further 2 minutes. When ready to serve, stir through the crème fraîche and season with freshly ground pepper.

(continues)

Grape-glazed duck *continued*

At the same time, melt the butter for the beans in a second frying pan. Add the beans and brine, season with salt and pepper and cook to heat through before adding the lemon juice and zest. Fry off a bit of the moisture, then when the beans start to turn golden, lightly crush with a fork. Add a little water if they're looking dry and season to taste. The total cooking time should be about 4–4½ minutes.

Slice the duck into thick slices, 2–3cm (¾–1in) thick, with a very sharp knife. Rest again while you make the glaze. Add the grape jelly to the pan with the reserved duck fat and bring to a gentle boil over a medium heat for about 1 minute, stirring the sugars and fats together.

Plate up the butter beans first, place the duck slices on top and drizzle over some of the glaze. Serve the greens on the side. Pour the remaining glaze into a little jug, in case you need more.

Notes
- Try different jellies you might have for your glaze: plum, quince, apple, medlar, rhubarb, blackcurrant or redcurrant.
- If you have no jelly to hand in your condiment ghost-town then duck matches beautifully with orange, so try with a marmalade instead.

New Zealand pavlova with marmalade

When I grew up in the '80s, pavlova was showcased on many a celebratory table. Classically, the billowing pillow of softness with its slightly crunchy exterior would be topped with lightly whipped cream, freshly sliced strawberries, passionfruit and kiwi fruit, maybe a little grated milk chocolate if we were lucky.

Pavlova shouldn't have a chewy inside. It's not merely a meringue with cream on top as some recipes might have you think. It should be melt-in-your-mouth soft with a gentle bite to the surface, much like the Russian ballerina it was named after.

As traditions evolve, so has my palate. These days, I like to add citrus, like marmalade, to my pavs and dress them with dehydrated fruits or vegetables and toasted nuts.

Serves 6–8

4 large free-range egg whites,
    at room temperature
225g (1 cup plus 2 Tbsp) caster
    (superfine) sugar
1 tsp vanilla extract
1 tsp white wine vinegar
2 tsp cornflour (cornstarch)

To serve
200ml (generous ¾ cup) double
    (heavy) cream, whipped
3–4 Tbsp Clementine and Whisky
    Marmalade (page 128), loosened
    with 2 tsp water
handful of pistachios or toasted
    almonds, roughly chopped
dehydrated carrot twists and orange
    peel discs (page 210) (optional)

Preheat the oven to 160°C (140°C fan/325°F/gas mark 3).

Draw out a 20–21cm (8in) diameter circle on a large sheet of baking paper and place on a baking sheet.

In a stand mixer fitted with the whisk attachment or in a large bowl with an electric hand whisk, whisk the egg whites on high speed until light and fluffy, at least 4 minutes. Reduce the speed and add 1 tablespoon of the sugar at a time, whisking to dissolve the sugar each time before adding another. Beat for 10 minutes after the last of the sugar goes in, until it's glossy with very stiff peaks. Be diligent with this beating time for better results.

Add the vanilla, vinegar and cornflour and mix on a slow speed until combined. Sprinkle the baking sheet with a little water and spoon or pipe the meringue mixture within the circle shape. Build the meringue up, even out the top and using a spoon make a few peaks as you go to give it some texture.

Reduce the oven heat to 120°C (100°C fan/250°F/gas mark ½) and bake the meringue for 70 minutes, then turn off the oven and leave cooling inside for at least another 3 hours or overnight. Do not be tempted to open the oven door during this time.

When ready to serve, top the pavlova with the whipped cream, drizzle over the loosened marmalade and sprinkle on the pistachios or toasted almonds. I like to add dehydrated carrot shavings and sometimes dehydrated citrus or fresh zest.

Notes
- The pavlova can be kept, covered, at room temperature for up to 1-2 days before decorating.
- If using frozen egg whites, make sure you defrost them first in the fridge for at least 4-5 hours.
- Substitute the marmalade for any other you have, or a stone-fruit jam or curd will be equally delicious. I've made this pavlova using a carrot marmalade and a peach jam.
- Caramelize the nuts if you want a sweeter version and have fun with dehydrating fruits or vegetables, such as sliced pineapple, limes, blood oranges, apples, pears, beetroot (beets) or parsnips (page 210).

Notes
- Substitute the marmalade for any other you may have, omit the poppy seeds and mix the seeds from a vanilla pod through the sugar instead.
- You can make one larger pudding using the same technique, steaming it for about 1½ hours.
- These can be made and kept in the fridge for 2-3 days (or frozen and defrosted). Just re-steam them for 10-15 minutes to warm through.

Lemon and poppy-seed steamed puddings with crème anglaise

Steaming is an alternative to baking, giving you a pudding that's full of moisture. It's a different type of baking and I want to give you a variety of inspiration. This is my take on a "Paddington Bear" steamed pudding, using lemons instead of oranges as my bitter element.

Serves 4

100g (scant ½ cup) unsalted butter, at room temperature, plus extra for greasing
70g (⅓ cup) light brown sugar
2 large free-range eggs, at room temperature
40g (3 Tbsp) Greek-style yoghurt
130g (1 cup) self-raising (self-rising) flour
¼ tsp baking powder
pinch of sea salt
zest and juice of 1 lemon
1 tsp poppy seeds
milk, if needed
8 heaped tsp Lemon and Poppy-seed Marmalade (page 129)

To serve
400ml (1¾ cups) thin custard or Crème Anglaise (page 207) or double (heavy) cream

Grease 4 small pudding moulds/basins or ramekins, about 7.5cm (3in) in diameter, each holding 150ml (⅔ cup). Cut out 4 baking paper discs to fit just inside the rim of your moulds and lightly grease one side. Cut 4 squares of foil that are big enough to make a domed hat over the top of the moulds.

In a stand mixer fitted with the paddle attachment, or with an electric hand whisk, cream the butter and sugar until pale and fluffy. Mix in 1 egg at a time, fully incorporating each time before adding the next, then slowly mix through the yoghurt.

In a separate bowl, mix together the flour, baking powder, salt, lemon zest and poppy seeds. Add a large spoonful at a time to the wet ingredients, mixing until just combined, until you have a smooth batter, then stir through the lemon juice and a little milk to loosen the mixture if it's too stiff.

Fill each pudding mould with 2 heaped teaspoons of marmalade, then equally distribute the batter among the moulds. Smooth down the tops with a spatula and place a paper disc on top of each, greased-side down, touching the entire surface. Cover each mould with a domed foil hat, securing with kitchen string or an elastic band to make them watertight.

Boil a large kettle of water. Place the moulds in a large saucepan and pour in enough boiling water to reach three-quarters of the way up the sides of the moulds. Cover the pan with the lid and steam over a medium-high heat for 30–35 minutes. Keep an eye on the water level, topping it up when necessary. They should rise slightly and spring to the touch – they are ready when an inserted skewer comes out clean.

Meanwhile, make your crème anglaise, if using.

When the puddings are ready, use oven gloves to turn them upside down onto a plate, releasing them from their moulds. The marmalade should dribble down the sides. Serve with warm crème anglaise or cream.

Pineapple, lime and tequila marmalade trifles

Trifles always seem to be made on special occasions, like Christmas. That one special large glass bowl you have in storage is carefully carried out to the table filled to the brim with layers of sponge, fruit, custard, cream and a healthy dose of booze. It's time to bring this classic to an everyday, any-day occasion by serving them individually. Try this tropical version - it's light and perfect as a mid-summer treat.

Serves 4–6

Sponge fingers
30g (2 Tbsp) unsalted butter, softened, plus extra for greasing
30g (2½ Tbsp) caster (superfine) sugar
½ tsp vanilla extract
1 medium free-range egg, at room temperature, separated
30g (4 Tbsp) self-raising (self-rising) flour
½ tsp baking powder
20g (3 Tbsp) ground almonds or almond flour
pinch of sea salt
milk, if needed
15g (3 Tbsp) flaked (slivered) almonds

Trifle
3–4 pineapple rings (canned are okay)
1 Tbsp Demerara or brown sugar
100g (⅓ cup) Lime and Tequila Marmalade (page 129)
60ml (¼ cup) tequila
500ml (generous 2 cups) thick vanilla custard or Crème Pâtissière (page 206)
150ml (⅔ cup) double (heavy) cream, lightly whipped
30g (6 Tbsp) flaked (slivered) almonds, lightly toasted
finely grated zest of 1 lime

The sponge fingers can be made a few days ahead, as it's better when they get a little dry and stale. Preheat the oven to 200°C (180°C fan/400°F/gas mark 6). Line and grease a 9 x 19cm (1lb) loaf pan, or a 16–18cm (6½–7in) diameter cake pan.

In a stand mixer fitted with the paddle attachment, or with an electric hand whisk, cream the butter and sugar together on medium speed for 5 minutes until pale and fluffy. Add the vanilla and egg yolk, mixing slowly until combined. Sift in the flour and baking powder, then fold through the ground almonds and salt. Whisk the egg white separately to soft peaks, then fold it through the mixture. The cake batter should be light and loose – only add milk if it looks too stiff.

Pour the batter into the prepared pan and sprinkle with the almonds. Bake in the middle of the oven for 10–12 minutes until spongy to the touch and an inserted toothpick comes out clean. Remove from the pan and cool on a wire rack.

When cool, slice into 9 x 2cm (3½ x ¾in) rectangular fingers and store in an airtight container until ready to use.

For the trifle, if you are making the custard yourself, make it in advance and chill in the fridge.

Sprinkle the pineapple rings with the sugar. Place under a preheated grill (broiler) for 3–4 minutes, charring each side, or use a griddle pan. Chop into small, bite-sized pieces.

(continues)

Pineapple and marmalade trifles *continued*

Roughly tear 4–5 sponge fingers and divide equally among the bottom of 4–6 individual 250ml (8½fl oz) glass bowls, or arrange in the bottom of one large glass serving bowl.

Mix the marmalade with the tequila and pour over the sponge fingers until they are equally soaked, reserving some to drizzle on later. Evenly divide the pineapple chunks among the bowls. Spoon on the custard, leaving room for the final layer, and chill until ready to serve.

Serve, topped with the whipped cream and a drizzle of the reserved marmalade syrup, decorated with the toasted almonds and the lime zest.

Notes
- The sponge fingers can be stored in an airtight container in the fridge for up to 10 days, it doesn't matter if they get harder in texture.
- Work this seasonally and substitute any marmalade you have with another or use a jam. Mix in other alcohols, such as orange with Cointreau or apricot with amaretto. Berry jams work too - try raspberry and brandy, or strawberry and Pimm's.

Coconut layer cake with lime and tequila marmalade and cream-cheese frosting

This cake, although layered and smothered in cream-cheese frosting, remains light and full of flavour. This is a way to showcase marmalade as a glaze for a cake. What better way than to match lime, tequila and coconut together to create complexity and intrigue and a tropical holiday feel. It's also a great opportunity to use up a lot of egg whites you might have stored in your freezer after making multiple custards and ice creams.

Serves 8–10

90g (⅓ cup plus 1 Tbsp) unsalted butter, softened, plus extra for greasing
90ml (⅓ cup) rapeseed (canola) or light vegetable oil
350g (1¾ cups) caster (superfine) sugar
200g (scant 1 cup) soured cream
2 tsp vanilla extract
350g (2⅔ cups) plain white (all-purpose) flour
1 tsp baking powder
½ tsp bicarbonate of soda (baking soda)
½ tsp sea salt
40g (generous ½ cup) desiccated (dried grated) coconut
6 medium free-range egg whites

Marmalade glaze
150g (generous ½ cup) Lime and Tequila Marmalade (page 129)
60ml (¼ cup) just-boiled water

Frosting
400g (1¾ cups) unsalted butter, cubed, at room temperature
100g (¾ cup) icing (confectioners') sugar
small pinch of sea salt
500g (1lb 2oz) cream cheese, at room temperature
20g (4½ Tbsp) desiccated (dried grated) coconut

To decorate
15g (⅓ cup) shaved coconut, lightly toasted
dehydrated lime discs (page 210) and lime zest (optional)

Preheat the oven to 200°C (180°C fan/400°F/gas mark 6). Cut out and grease 6 x 19cm (7½in) circles of baking paper. Grease and line the base of 3 springform cake pans of the same size, setting aside the 3 remaining baking paper circles.

In a stand mixer fitted with the paddle attachment, or with an electric hand whisk, cream the butter, oil and sugar together for at least 5 minutes until pale and fluffy. Add the soured cream and vanilla and gently mix in.

In a separate bowl, sift together the flour, baking powder, bicarbonate of soda and salt, then stir through the desiccated coconut. Fold into the butter mixture, one large spoonful at a time, using a spatula to gently combine.

Whisk the egg whites to stiff peaks, 4–5 minutes. Fold into the batter, one large spoonful at a time, trying not to lose too much air but combining thoroughly.

Evenly divide the batter among the cake pans, even out the tops with a spatula and make a dip in the middle of each. Gently place the reserved paper discs on top, greased side down, covering the surface of each. Bake for 8–10 minutes or until an inserted skewer comes out clean. Remove from the pans and leave to cool completely on a wire rack.

Make the glaze. In a small saucepan, stir together the marmalade and hot water over a medium heat until it boils and becomes syrupy. Drizzle and brush the glaze evenly over the top of the 3 cake layers.

(continues)

Coconut layer cake *continued*

To make the frosting, use an electric whisk to cream the butter, icing sugar and salt together until very light and fluffy. Add 2 tablespoons of the cream cheese and beat in at a high speed, removing any lumps. Then, slowly fold through the remaining cream cheese with a spatula. Finally, fold through the coconut until combined.

Assemble the cake by spreading a thick layer of frosting between the cake layers and stacking them on top of one another. Continue to spread the frosting around the sides and top until entirely covered. Dress the cake with coconut flakes and dehydrated lime discs or zest.

Notes
- If you only have 1 or 2 cake pans, it is fine for the batter to sit and wait between baking the layers, if all done within the hour.
- The cake layers can be kept in airtight containers for 1-2 days before assembling and icing. Eat within 2-3 days once iced and keep in the fridge due to the cream cheese.
- Substitute any marmalade you have with another or a jam, keeping within the flavour profile of coconut: try coconut and orange, coconut and raspberry, coconut and peach, or coconut and apricot.

Peanut butter and jelly chocolate cups

One for the American kid in me, which probably comes from New Zealand TV in the '80s, where we had a mixture of programmes from the UK and the US, with a little bit of what we call "Kiwiana" brought in here and there. With peanut butter and jelly being a classic American combination, I couldn't pass bringing these two American "flavourites" together, for a fun, easy, '80s-style chocolate treat.

Makes 14 cups

70g (¼ cup) smooth peanut butter
    or almond butter
2 Tbsp icing (confectioners') sugar
210g (7½oz) milk chocolate
    (37 per cent cocoa solids)
50–60g (3 Tbsp) Grape Jelly
    (page 130)

In a small pan, warm the peanut butter with the icing sugar over a low heat, stirring to combine and allowing the sugar to melt into the butter.

Melt the chocolate in a bowl set over a pan of simmering water (ensure the bottom of the bowl does not touch the water), stirring intermittently until smooth.

Place 1½ teaspoons of the melted chocolate into 14 mini cupcake cups. I use 5cm/20ml (¾in/¾fl oz) silicone cups, but paper muffin cases work well, too. Gently swirl each cup so some of the chocolate coats the sides a little.

Carefully spoon ¾ teaspoon of the peanut butter into the middle of each cup, then add ½ teaspoon of grape jelly to each. Spoon a further 1½ teaspoons of melted chocolate on top. Place on a tray and chill in the fridge for at least 1–2 hours until set.

Notes
- Try different jellies you might have: damson, plum, quince, apple, medlar, blackberry.
- Or try jams: raspberry, strawberry, apricot.
- Different chocolates work as well: dark with 70 per cent cocoa solids, or white chocolate.

Recipes to make from scratch

Recipes to make your daily cooking as sustainable as possible. Included here are a few things to make from scratch, like breads, cheeses, cured fish and mayonnaise, but also how to make the most of any by-products from one recipe to another. By all means, buy these from your local supplier, but you'll be surprised how easy it is to whip some of these things up with staple ingredients you might already have.

Flatbread

Makes 8

400g (3 cups) self-raising
 (self-rising) flour, plus extra
 for dusting
½ tsp sea salt
200g (scant 1 cup) plain yoghurt
 or buttermilk
70ml (5 Tbsp) lukewarm water
1 Tbsp olive oil
2 tsp za'atar or toasted cumin seeds

Mix together the flour and salt in a bowl.

In a separate large bowl, mix together the yoghurt, water and oil. Pour in the dry ingredients and mix into a soft dough that's not too sticky. Divide the dough into 8 equal portions.

Sprinkle the work surface with the spices. Knead and roll out each piece of dough into a large, flat oval shape, about 5mm (¼in) thick, dusting with a little extra flour.

Heat a dry cast-iron griddle pan, comal or heavy-based frying pan, or place a baking sheet under the grill (broiler) until very hot. Cook the flatbreads in the pan or on the baking sheet for 1–3 minutes on each side until slightly golden and puffed up. Keep the cooked ones wrapped in a clean dish towel in a very low oven while cooking the rest and serve warm.

Note
- Paprika and crushed toasted coriander seeds make a delicious substitute for the za'atar or cumin. Try other things, too, such as turmeric and crushed peppercorns, or nigella seeds with fenugreek.

Wholemeal chapattis

Makes 8

120g (scant 1 cup) wholemeal
 (wholewheat) flour
120g (scant 1 cup) plain (all-purpose)
 flour, plus extra for dusting
1 tsp sea salt
2 Tbsp light olive oil, plus extra
 for greasing
140ml (scant ⅔ cup) hot water,
 plus extra if needed

In a large bowl, mix together the flours and salt and stir in the oil. Slowly add the water, a little at a time, until it becomes a soft dough, not too sticky.

Knead the dough on a dusted work surface for about 8 minutes until smooth and glossy. Divide the dough into 8 equal portions, roll into balls and leave to rest for 5 minutes.

Roll the balls into very thin, large rounds, about 1mm (1/32in) thick and 18cm (7in) in diameter.

Heat a large, very lightly oiled frying pan or a dry cast-iron skillet over a very high heat. Cook each chapatti, one at a time, for about 30 seconds on each side, adjusting the heat accordingly, until puffed up with brown patches. Make sure you grease the frying pan, if using, between chapattis and keep the cooked ones wrapped in a clean dish towel in a very low oven while cooking the rest.

Notes
- Try these at breakfast to wrap up bacon, a fried egg, spinach, with a chutney or homemade tomato sauce.
- This dough freezes really well, so if you find you only need 2–4 chapattis for your dinner, freeze the dough balls and defrost them fully before rolling out when you need them.

Crumpets

Makes 6–8

15g (1½ Tbsp) dried active yeast
240ml (1 cup) lukewarm milk,
    30–40°C (86–104°F), plus
    extra if needed
240g (1¾ cups) plain (all-purpose)
    or strong bread flour
1 tsp sea salt
2 tsp white or golden caster
    (superfine) sugar
½ tsp bicarbonate of soda (baking
    soda) dissolved in 80ml (⅓ cup)
    water
1½ Tbsp unsalted butter, melted and
    cooled
vegetable oil, for greasing

Mix the yeast with the milk in a small bowl and let it stand for 5–6 minutes while it activates. Stir it as it becomes slightly frothy.

With an electric whisk or stand mixer fitted with the paddle attachment, mix together the flour, salt and sugar, then add the yeasted milk, soda-infused water and cooled butter. Mix at medium speed for about 3–5 minutes until there are no lumps. It should be like a batter; add more milk if you feel it's a bit heavy. Cover with a clean dish towel and leave to prove at room temperature (ideally 20–22°C/68–72°F) for 30–60 minutes until the batter looks bubbly and has doubled in size. Place in the fridge for the last 10 minutes.

Lightly grease a frying pan or cast-iron skillet with oil, along with six 9cm (3½in) crumpet rings, and place the rings in the pan over a medium heat to heat up. Reduce the heat to low and ladle enough batter into the rings to fill them halfway. Gently cook for 8–10 minutes until bubbles have appeared and popped and they are cooked all the way up to the top. Traditionally, they are cooled at this stage and toasted later, but if you want to eat them immediately, flip them over and gently toast the tops in the pan for 1–2 minutes until browned.

English muffins

Makes 6–8

6g (2 tsp) dried active yeast
140ml (scant ⅔ cup) lukewarm milk,
    30–40°C (86–104°F), plus extra
    if needed
320g (scant 2½ cups) plain
    (all-purpose) flour, plus extra
    for dusting
1 tsp sea salt
2½ tsp white or raw caster
    (superfine) sugar
1 medium free-range egg, lightly
    beaten
40g (3 Tbsp) Greek-style plain
    yoghurt
2 tsp unsalted butter, softened
vegetable oil, for greasing
semolina/polenta, for dusting

Mix the yeast with the milk in a small bowl and let it stand for 5–6 minutes while it activates. Stir so it becomes frothy.

In a large bowl or stand mixer fitted with the paddle attachment, mix together the flour, salt and sugar, then add the yeasted milk along with the egg, yoghurt and butter, and mix until combined, about 5 minutes. Add more milk if you feel it's a bit dry.

Change to the hook attachment on the stand mixer or hand knead the dough for 5–10 minutes. The dough should be soft and shaggy, unlike firmer bread doughs. Lightly grease a large bowl, place the dough in it, cover and leave to prove at room temperature (ideally 20–22°C/ 68–72°F) for at least 1 hour until doubled in size.

Lightly dust the work surface with semolina and flour and roll out the dough to about 2cm (¾in) thick. Cut out about 6–8 circles with a 9cm (3½in) cutter. If you like, place the muffins into lightly greased 9cm (3½in) diameter crumpet/egg rings (I find this helps the shape later, but it's not essential) and place on a semolina-dusted baking sheet. Dust the tops with semolina and leave to prove for a further 30 minutes.

Preheat a dry cast-iron skillet or frying pan until hot, then reduce the heat to low. Slip the muffins out of the rings, if used, and cook 3–4 at a time for 4–6 minutes on each side.

Lucy May's scones

When I think about my nan, I fondly think of her scones. Nan's were always perfect and she would whip them up in 15-20 minutes. I wish I had spent more time in the kitchen with her learning this invaluable skill, but with 24 grandchildren there was not a lot of lone scone teaching.

I asked my Auntie Cher for the magic, but she told me Nan never had a recipe - they were made by look and feel - so this is relayed the best she could. This idea, that recipes are passed down by sight and feel from one home cook to another, with no written testimony, is one that I love. A familiar sentiment to us all.

Makes 8 large or 16 small

250g (scant 2 cups) plain (all-purpose) flour, or light spelt, plus extra for dusting
4 tsp baking powder
½ tsp sea salt
50g (3½ Tbsp) unsalted butter, cold, cubed
150ml milk, plus extra for brushing
2 Tbsp warm water, or as needed

Preheat the oven to 230°C (210°C fan/450°F/gas mark 8). Lightly dust a baking sheet with some flour or line with baking paper.

Combine the flour, baking powder and salt in a large bowl. You get the best results by hand-mixing these, as you won't overwork the dough and it's just as quick. Rub in the cold butter between your fingertips until it resembles fine breadcrumbs. Mix the milk with the warm water to take off the chill and add to the bowl, mixing quickly with a butter knife. This will make a softer dough – it's important not to overwork it. It should be soft and slightly tacky but not wet. Only add more milk to get it to the right consistency.

When the dough just comes together, turn out onto a board very lightly dusted with flour. Shape into a rough rectangle, 18 x 10cm (7 x 4in) and about 5cm (2in) thick. With the longest side facing you, cut it in half, then cut each half into quarters (8 rectangles) or diagonally again for smaller triangle scones.

Place the scones on your baking sheet, 2cm (¾in) apart, and brush the tops with milk. Bake in the middle of the oven for 12–14 minutes until golden brown.

Allow to cool for a few minutes before removing from the baking sheet. Serve warm or cold with your choice of seasonal jam and whipped cream, or just with butter and jam like we ate them at Nan's.

Notes
- For flavour additions, add 60-80g (about ½ cup) raisins/sultanas (golden raisins), chopped dates or chocolate chips to the dry ingredients.
- If it's cheesy scones you want, add 100-150g (1-1½ cups) grated mature Cheddar cheese or red Leicester with 1 teaspoon of mustard powder and a small pinch of cayenne pepper, and grate some cheese on top.
- Grill a chopped slice of bacon and/or caramelize a red onion and stir it through the wet mix.
- Use chopped chives, spring onions (scallions) or even pickled jalapeños and add to the mix.

Pikelets/drop scones

Makes 10–20

125g (scant 1 cup) plain (all-purpose) or buckwheat flour, or light spelt
1 tsp baking powder
pinch of sea salt
50g (¼ cup) white or golden caster (superfine) sugar
1 medium free-range egg, lightly beaten
150ml (⅔ cup) milk (regular, oat or almond), plus extra if needed
vegetable oil or butter, for greasing

Sift the flour into a large bowl with the baking powder and salt, and stir through the sugar. Make a well in the middle and add the egg and a quarter of the milk and use a fork to stir, gently mixing the dry into the wet. Keep adding the milk in quarters until well combined, then use a hand whisk to beat out any lumps to make a smooth, runny batter that resembles a thickened cream. Add more milk, if needed. Stir through any flavour additions (see below), then cover and refrigerate for 10–20 minutes.

Lightly grease a heavy-based frying pan or cast-iron skillet and heat over a medium-high heat. When sizzling, reduce the heat slightly and add about 1 tablespoon of the batter to make a pikelet. Cook in batches of 3–4 pikelets at a time, keeping in mind that they will spread out. Cook for 1–2 minutes until they start to bubble on the surface and then pop, then flip and cook the other side for about 1 minute.

Serve warm or cold with softened butter and your choice of seasonal jam. Great for breakfast, brunch or afternoon tea.

Notes
- Flavour additions: 1-2 tsp of either blueberry powder, cinnamon, drinking chocolate, chopped almonds, chocolate chips, cacao nibs, oats, raisins, cherries, or blueberries, etc.

Hokkaido milk burger buns/ Japanese brioche

I have to thank one of my favourite London chefs for sharing this Japanese milk bread recipe with me, when I was struggling to find the perfect burger bun for my Kiwi burgers. Chris Leach, thank you for sharing your knowledge.

This milk bread is a type of Japanese brioche, but less buttery. You make up a roux called a *tangzhong*, which is then added to the yeasted dough, making for a very light, fluffy, milky bread.

Makes 6 buns (or 1 loaf)

Tangzhong
20g (2 Tbsp plus 1 tsp) strong bread flour
4 Tbsp milk
2 Tbsp water

Buns/loaf
9g (2½ tsp) fast-action dried yeast
120ml (½ cup) lukewarm milk, 30–40°C (86–104°F)
325g (2⅓ cups) strong bread flour, plus extra for dusting
½ tsp sea salt

First, make the tangzhong. Whisk the ingredients in a small saucepan over a medium-low heat for 2–3 minutes until it thickens, like a roux might, without any lumps. Allow to cool to room temperature.

For the buns/loaf, add the yeast to the lukewarm milk and leave to activate for 5–6 minutes, then gently stir to dissolve.

In a large bowl, or in a stand mixer fitted with the hook attachment, mix together the flour, salt and sugar. Slowly add the yeasted milk, then the tangzhong and the egg and yolk. Mix at a low speed for about 4–5 minutes. Increase the speed to medium-low and

(continues)

45g (scant ¼ cup) white or golden caster (superfine) sugar
1 large free-range egg plus 1 large yolk
55g (scant ¼ cup) butter, at room temperature, cubed
vegetable oil, for greasing

To finish
1 egg lightly beaten with 1 Tbsp milk, for egg wash
2–3 tsp sesame seeds or poppy seeds (optional)

slowly add the butter, a little at a time. When the butter is fully incorporated, reduce the speed to low and knead for about 8 minutes. If doing by hand, knead the butter into the dough on a lightly dusted work surface for 10–15 minutes until the dough is smooth and elastic.

Scrape the dough into a large bowl very lightly greased with oil, cover the bowl with a clean dish towel and leave to prove in a warm place for 60–90 minutes until the dough has puffed up and doubled in size.

Punch down into the middle of the raised dough and portion into about 6 pieces (about 110g/4oz each). Roll the balls under a cupped hand, making swift circular motions to create perfectly round buns. Place the buns, 5cm (2in) apart, on a lightly floured large baking sheet, cover and leave to prove for 40–60 minutes until they have puffed up to the desired shape and size.

Meanwhile, preheat the oven to 200°C (180°C fan/ 400°F/gas mark 6).

Brush the buns with egg wash and sprinkle with the sesame or poppy seeds, if using. Bake in the middle of the oven for 16–20 minutes until golden on top and cooked through.

Best eaten within 2 days, but can be frozen and defrosted for later use.

Notes
- Perfect as a bun for Kiwi Burgers (page 20), or made into a loaf for slicing for a PBJ (page 102) or bread and butter pudding.
- To make this into a loaf, after the first prove, mould the dough into a rectangle on a lightly floured surface. Cut down 3 slits and braid the strands before placing it into a lightly greased loaf pan to prove for the second time. The loaf will need 18-22 minutes of baking time.

Croutons or breadcrumbs

any stale bread

Any bread that goes stale over time can be made into croutons or breadcrumbs and stored in the freezer in an airtight container. Simply cut the stale slices into 1cm (½in) cubes, bake for 15–20 minutes in a 140°C (120°C fan/275°F/gas mark 1) oven.

Sprinkle with sea salt if making croutons. For breadcrumbs, leave unsalted and blitz the cubes in a food processor to the crumb size you desire.

Corn tortillas

Makes 10–12

220g (scant 2 cups) masa harina
    or fine corn (maize) flour, plain
    or blue, plus extra if needed
1 tsp sea salt dissolved in 300ml
    (1¼ cups) very warm water (or
    240ml/1 cup if using blue flour)

Put the flour into a large bowl and slowly mix through 280ml (scant 1¼ cups) of the warm salty water (220ml/ scant 1 cup if using blue flour). It should be a bit gritty and lumpy. Leave for 6–8 minutes.

Squeeze the mixture into a dough and knead for about 5 minutes until it becomes smoother and more pliable. If you think it looks a little dry or too wet, add water or more flour – it should be like dry modelling clay, firm and springy but not too sticky. In my experience, it's better to be on the drier side rather than wetter.

Heat a cast-iron griddle pan, comal or skillet on a high heat.

Pinch off and weigh out 37g (1¼oz) pieces of dough, roll into balls in cupped palms and cover with a damp dish towel. Press each ball in a taco press between 2 pieces of baking paper or plastic (like a cut-up sandwich bag). Press once, then turn 180° and press again firmly, to get a more even thickness. If you don't have a press, gently squash with the palm of your hand and roll between baking paper/ plastic with a rolling pin, rotating and rolling to about 10–12cm (4½in) in diameter and about 2mm (1⁄16in) thick. To remove from the paper/plastic, pick up and peel off one side, flip the uncovered side onto the palm of your hand and gently peel back the rest. If it sticks to the paper/ plastic then your dough may be too wet. It helps to wipe it down with a damp cloth in between presses.

I like to press and cook 2–3 wraps at a time. That way, I can press 2–3 more while they are cooking, and avoid stacking (as they can stick together).

Cook the tortillas, 2–3 at a time, for 1–1½ minutes on each side, depending on the heat of your pan. They should be golden brown with air pockets and the odd burn knot might appear as the pan gets hotter. Once one side is cooked you can press down on it with a very damp folded dish towel, as the steam creates air pockets. Keep warm wrapped in a clean dry dish towel while cooking the rest.

Serve immediately. Alternatively, refrigerate, or freeze and defrost, then reheat in a low oven.

Buckwheat and pumpkin-seed crackers

Makes 15–20

90g (⅔ cup) buckwheat flour,
    plus extra if needed
60g (⅔ cup) ground almonds
    or almond flour
1 Tbsp ground flaxseed
½ tsp sea salt, plus extra to taste
freshly ground black pepper, to taste
1½ Tbsp olive oil
70ml (5 Tbsp) water, plus extra if
    needed
20g (2 Tbsp) shelled roasted
    pumpkin seeds

Preheat the oven to 200°C (180°C fan/400°F/gas mark 6).

In a large bowl, mix together all the dry ingredients except for the pumpkin seeds and create a well in the middle.

In a separate bowl, whisk together the oil and water and pour into the middle of the well. With a wooden spoon, gently mix the wet with the dry, let the dry fall into the wet a little at a time, stirring until thoroughly combined. Once it comes together, knead on a flat surface for 2–3 minutes until the dough becomes smooth with a slight gloss to it. Add a little extra water or flour, if needed, so that it's not too tacky yet not too dry. Roll into a ball, cut in half, then roll each half into a ball.

Separately roll out each ball with a rolling pin between 2 large sheets of baking paper until about 1mm (¹⁄₃₂in) thick (the thinner the better), resembling a pizza base. Peel off the top layer of paper and sprinkle half the pumpkin seeds over each along with a healthy pinch of sea salt. Replace the paper and roll once more, pressing in the seeds, then remove the top layer of paper. Score the dough into wedges, triangles, squares, or shapes of your choice and prick each shape with a fork a few times. Transfer on the bottom sheet of paper to a baking sheet.

Bake in the middle of the oven for 10–15 minutes until golden. Keep an eye on them as different ovens cook at different rates and you don't want to burn the edges. Move them while cooking to let them cook evenly.

Let cool and snap apart. Store in an airtight container for up to 1 week.

Note
- Mix up and use your own flavour pairings, such as rosemary and Parmesan or sunflower-seeded buckwheat crackers. Smoked paprika and sage make an interesting pairing, too. Alternatively, add a little sugar or honey with lemon zest for a sweeter version.

Gyoza wrappers

Makes 30–34 wrappers

190g (scant 1½ cups) plain
    (all-purpose) flour
¼ tsp sea salt dissolved in
    100–120ml (generous ⅓–½ cup)
    just-boiled water
cornflour (cornstarch) or flour,
    for dusting

Sift the flour into a large bowl. Slowly pour in the salted water, little by little, and stir with a wooden spoon until it starts to become a dough. You may not need all the water. Use your hands to finish, rolling the dough into a ball. Transfer to a work surface and knead for about 10 minutes until smoother in texture. Cut in half, roll each half into a log, then wrap each in a lightly damp cloth and rest for 30 minutes.

Sprinkle the work surface with a little cornflour or flour. Cut off 15 discs from each log. Cover the dough with a damp cloth while you work and roll out each disc using a rolling pin, turning and rotating, until you get an 8cm (3in) diameter circle about 3mm (⅛in) thick. Repeat with all discs. If you want a perfect circle, use a cookie cutter of a similar size to cut the shape out. Sprinkle each wrapper with a little cornflour and stack, covered with a lightly damp cloth to prevent them drying out.

Use immediately, or refrigerate for 3–4 days until ready to use. Alternatively, freeze for up to 1–2 months in an airtight container and defrost before using.

Homemade mustard

Makes about 180g (¾ cup)

55g (6 Tbsp) yellow mustard seeds
70ml (scant ⅓ cup) white wine
    vinegar
70ml (scant ⅓ cup) filtered water,
    or as needed
1 tsp honey, or more to taste
pinch of sea salt

Mix all the ingredients in a small non-reactive bowl and cover with waxed fabric, muslin (cheesecloth) or baking paper secured with kitchen string or an elastic band. Leave to stand for 2–3 days.

After this time, blend everything together to a smooth paste, dribbling in a little extra water if the consistency needs loosening up.

Store in a clean, sealed jar in the fridge for up to 6 months, but it's best eaten within 3–4 weeks.

Notes
- To make wholegrain mustard, use a blend of brown and yellow mustard seeds. Blend half, then stir through the other half whole.
- Replace the water with beer, wine or prosecco to play around with different flavour combinations.

Pickle-brine salad dressing

Makes about 110ml (scant ½ cup)

3 Tbsp any pickle brine
4 Tbsp olive oil
1 tsp wholegrain or Dijon mustard
2 tsp honey
a squeeze of lemon juice
sea salt and black pepper to taste

Use any of your leftover pickle brines to make a salad dressing. Just give all the ingredients a good shake or whisk in a jar or a bowl and it should create great coverage for any fresh mixed leaves you have to dress. Store in the fridge until ready to use.

Mayonnaise

Makes about 300g (scant 1½ cups)

1 large free-range egg yolk, at room
    temperature, or 4 Tbsp aquafaba
    for plant-based version
100ml (generous ⅓ cup) sunflower
    oil or other mild-flavoured oil
½ tsp Dijon mustard
pinch of sea salt
pinch of caster (superfine) sugar
2–3 Tbsp light-flavoured vinegar
120ml (½ cup) light olive oil
juice of about ½ lemon, or to taste

In a large bowl, whisk the egg yolk by hand or using a hand-held electric whisk. Slowly drizzle in the sunflower oil, whisking as you go so that it doesn't split, until it thickens and lightens in colour. Add the mustard, salt, sugar and vinegar, and continue whisking until it thickens up again. Slowly add the light olive oil in the same way as the sunflower oil. Squeeze in the lemon juice, to taste, and give it a final whisk so it is completely combined.

Store in a clean glass jar in the fridge for up to 1 week.

Notes
- If your egg is too cold or too warm it will not emulsify. Make sure the egg is at room temperature (about 21-23°C/70-73°F).
- To make aïoli, whisk through 2 finely chopped or minced garlic cloves at the end.

Cashew mayonnaise (vegan)

Makes about 300g (scant 1½ cups)

130g (1 heaped cup) raw cashew nuts
3–4 Tbsp water, or more as needed
pinch of sea salt
freshly ground black pepper, to taste
pinch of caster (superfine) sugar
2–3 Tbsp apple cider vinegar
2 tsp good-quality olive oil
juice of ½ lemon or lime, or to taste

Put the cashews in a bowl with the water and leave to soak for 6–8 hours.

Drain and rinse the nuts, then transfer to a food processor along with the other ingredients except the citrus juice. Blend, squeezing in the citrus juice to taste and adding a little extra water, if needed, to help the consistency. Give it a final blitz until it is completely smooth.

Store in a clean glass jar or airtight container in the fridge for up to 1 week.

Pickle-brine mayonnaise

any pickle brine

Replace the vinegar in any of the above mayonnaise recipes with the same measure of pickle brine. Play around with different pickle brines you might have knocking around in the fridge. Taste them first to see if this is how you want to flavour your mayo. Chilli ones work really well.

Homemade labneh

Makes about 250–300g (generous 1–1¼ cups)

Savoury Labneh
400g (scant 2 cups) full-fat plain
    Greek yoghurt
1 tsp sea salt

Sweet Labneh
400g (scant 2 cups) full-fat plain
    Greek yoghurt
2 tsp raw honey or raw caster
    (superfine) sugar
½ tsp ground cinnamon or seeds
    scraped from ½ vanilla pod
    (optional)

Stir the salt or sugar, or other flavourings, through the yoghurt and place it in a muslin (cheesecloth). Fold or tie up the edges so it is fully enclosed and suspend the cloth over a jug or bowl for 2–3 hours, or overnight for a firmer texture. I tend to leave mine in the fridge overnight.

Eat immediately or keep in a sealed container in the fridge for up to 1 week.

Note
- If you want to add another flavour, try dried herbs or spices, such as chilli, dried oregano, cinnamon or even dried cranberries.

Homemade soft cheese (ricotta) and whey

You can buy ricotta, but it's really easy and fun to make this homemade version using only a handful of ingredients. You also get an amazing by-product - whey - which is incredibly versatile.

Makes about 200g (¾ cup) soft cheese and about 850ml (3½ cups) whey

1 litre (generous 4 cups) whole milk
pinch of sea salt
2 tsp distilled white or white wine
    vinegar
2 tsp freshly squeezed lemon juice

Combine the milk and salt in a large, heavy-based pan set over a medium-low heat. Stirring intermittently, gently bring it to just before a boil when small bubbles start to appear, or 85°C (185°F) on the digital thermometer. Remove from the heat and gently stir through the vinegar and lemon juice. Continue stirring for a few minutes while the curds start to form, then cover and leave to rest for 30–40 minutes.

After this time, strain through a colander lined with muslin (cheesecloth) set over a bowl to catch the liquid (whey). Let the ricotta sit like this, covered, for 40–60 minutes, depending on how firm you want it. To finish, lift the corners of the muslin and twist down to gently squeeze out any excess liquid.

Place the ricotta and the collected whey into separate containers and store in the fridge. The ricotta will keep for up to 2 weeks in an airtight container; however, it tastes better in the first 3 days. The whey will keep for up to 6 months sealed.

Notes
- It helps to have a digital thermometer for this recipe and some muslin for straining.
- Make sure you keep your whey and use it in different recipes throughout this book. It also freezes well if you don't think you will use it in 6 months. Cook potatoes, pulses and grains in it - you'll revel in the creamier texture they take on.

Homemade butter and buttermilk

Makes about 250g (generous 1 cup) butter and 200ml (generous ¾ cup) buttermilk

500ml (generous 2 cups) double (heavy) cream
pinch of sea salt (optional)

In a stand mixer fitted with the whisk attachment, whisk the cream with the salt, if desired, on the highest speed until it gets thicker and thicker. Eventually, it will start to resemble butter, becoming more yellow, stiffer and getting stuck in the whisk. It will separate into solids and liquid. The solids are the butter; the liquid is buttermilk.

Remove the solids from the whisk, then submerge them in a large bowl of cold water. Squeeze out any of the excess liquid and firmly shape into a ball. Remove from the water and shape into a butter block or roll into a log in baking paper. Chill in the fridge where the fats will solidify and harden.

Pour the buttermilk left in the stand mixer into an airtight container.

Both will keep in the fridge for up to 2–3 weeks. You can also freeze the buttermilk for up to 2 months.

Crème pâtissière – thick vanilla custard

Use this thicker custard for pies, tarts, doughnuts or trifle fillings, or just pour it over sticky toffee pudding or fruit crumble. Halve the recipe for less. Try infusing it with different flavours (see note opposite).

Serves 4–6 (makes about 600ml/ generous 2½ cups)

500ml (generous 2 cups) whole milk
100g (½ cup) caster (superfine) sugar
½ vanilla pod, split and seeds scraped
40g (6½ Tbsp) cornflour (cornstarch)
4 large free-range egg yolks

Gently stir the milk together with half of the sugar in a saucepan over a medium heat.

Add the vanilla seeds and pod. Bring to a simmer, keeping an eye on it, and remove from the heat just before it reaches a boil.

In a heatproof bowl, mix the remaining sugar with the cornflour and whisk in the egg yolks until pale and fluffy. Pour a little of the steaming hot milk at a time into the egg mixture, whisking well until thoroughly combined.

Remove the vanilla pod and pour the mixture back into the saucepan. Cook gently over a medium-low heat, whisking continuously for 5–10 minutes or longer until it thickens to a custard consistency.

Eat hot or cold, but cover the bowl if chilling so a skin doesn't form. Keep in the fridge for up to 1 week.

Crème anglaise – thin vanilla custard

Use this thinner custard for pouring on almost everything (pickled fruits, steamed puddings) or when making bread and butter pudding. Halve the recipe for less. Making it is a patience game, but the reward is grand. Try infusing it with different flavours (see note below).

Serves 4–5 (makes about 550ml/ 2⅓ cups)

250ml (generous 1 cup) whole milk
250ml (generous 1 cup) double (heavy) cream
½ vanilla pod, split and seeds scraped
60g (5 Tbsp) caster (superfine) sugar
3 large free-range egg yolks

Combine the milk, cream, vanilla seeds and pod and half of the sugar in a saucepan over a medium heat. Bring to a simmer, keeping an eye on it, and remove from the heat just before it reaches a boil.

In a heatproof bowl, whisk the remaining sugar with the egg yolks. Pour a little of the steaming hot milk at a time into the egg mixture, whisking well until thoroughly combined.

Pour the mixture back into the saucepan. Cook, whisking gently with a heart or magic whisk, over a medium-low heat for 5–10 minutes or longer until it reaches 82°C (180°F) on a digital thermometer. The custard is ready when it has slightly thickened and coats the back of a spoon.

Remove the vanilla pod and serve hot. Alternatively, cool in a bowl set over a bed of ice, then cover and refrigerate. Keep in the fridge for up to 1 week.

Notes
- All is not lost (in either custard) if the eggs look as if they may start to split and/or scramble. It means it's too hot. Remove to a cool bowl (sitting it in ice if you need to) and use a hand blender to smooth it out or, if this fails, try to sieve out any lumps.
- To add a different flavour, omit the vanilla and first warm the measure of milk with 10-40g (⅓-1½oz) of leaves, dried flowers or tea (depending on the strength you like and the strength of flavouring you are adding). Let it infuse for 1 hour before sieving and making either custard. Chamomile, lemon verbena, green tea, hibiscus, rose and fig leaf make lovely infusions.
- Alternatively, add very finely grated citrus zest at the end (lemon, lime or orange), or coffee grounds.
- Never throw out your egg whites - freeze them separately in an ice-cube tray so you know exactly how many to defrost in the fridge when you come to make Pavlova (page 178) or my Coconut Layer Cake (page 185).

Home-cured and smoked fish

To cure

Makes about 250g (9oz)

80g (generous ⅓ cup) caster (superfine) sugar
80g (⅓ cup) sea salt
1–2 fillets of trout, salmon or mackerel (about 250–300g/9–10½oz)
Optional flavourings: tea leaves, beetroot (beet) juice, dried herbs, gin

Mix together the sugar and salt in a bowl and pour half evenly over the bottom of a Tupperware container or dish that will snugly fit the fish. Place the fish, skin-side down, onto the sugar/salt bed and evenly sprinkle the remaining mixture over the flesh so that it's completely covered. Cover and refrigerate for at least 4–8 hours (depending on the thickness of your fish, it may need longer; however, you don't want it to be too salty).

Once cured, thoroughly wash off all of the sugar/salt under very cold running water. Pat dry with paper towels. You can leave the cured fish like this and slice very finely or go on to smoke it.

Slice off thin slivers with a sharp knife when you are ready to serve.

Note
- Experiment with the optional flavourings by adding them to the sugar/salt mix at the beginning.

To smoke

Makes about 250g (9oz)

1–2 fillets of trout, salmon or mackerel (about 250–300g/9–10½oz), fresh or cured as above
1 Tbsp oak or hickory chips

Put the wood chips in the middle of an outdoor smoker, spray or drizzle with very little water and light the chips. When you see smoke appear, cover with foil and place the fish fillets, skin-side down, onto the grate. Smoke for 8–10 minutes if using cured fillets and for 10–15 minutes if fresh.

If you have a stovetop smoker, follow the manufacturer's instructions. You may not need to drizzle the chips with water. Smoke over a medium-low heat for the same amount of time as above.

Note
- If you haven't got a smoker, you can fashion one. Line a steel baking sheet or a large pot with some foil. Add the chips, put another layer of foil on top of the chips and place a wire grate/rack, sieve or steamer that will fit inside. Place the fish, skin-side down, on this. Cover with a lid, sealing off any gaps with extra foil, and place on the stove top over a medium-low heat. Allow to smoke for 10–15 minutes.

Dukkah

Makes about 200g (1½ cups)

50g (⅓ cup) hazelnuts, dry roasted
50g (½ cup) almonds, dry roasted
50g (⅓ cup) sesame seeds
1 Tbsp coriander seeds
1 Tbsp cumin seeds
2 tsp fennel seeds
1 Tbsp dried thyme
½ tsp sea salt
freshly ground black pepper

Toast the hazelnuts and almonds in a dry frying pan over a medium-low heat, tossing frequently until you hear them start to crackle and you can smell them start to release their oils. You want to keep a keen eye that they don't get too brown and burn but rather turn golden. Dry and cool on a piece of paper towel.

Toast the sesame, coriander, cumin and fennel seeds in a dry frying pan and allow to cool.

Tip the nuts into a food processor and pulse 2–3 times until chopped (or chop into very small pieces).

Add the seeds to the processor and pulse another 2–3 times so it remains chunky and doesn't turn to paste (alternatively, crush them with a pestle and mortar). Mix the nuts and seeds together with the thyme, salt and a few grinds of pepper and store in an airtight container. It will keep for up 6 months sealed.

Dehydrated fruit and vegetables

I like to use these instead of fresh fruit for decorations on cakes or meringues, but they can work equally as well as a healthy snack for children. Once you start you won't be able to stop.

Fruit
apples, pears, oranges, limes, lemons, strawberries, kiwi fruit, bananas, mangoes, raspberries, coconut, pineapple, sliced into very fine discs or decorative shapes

Vegetables
carrots, beetroot (beets), parsnips or celery, finely sliced or cut into ribbons (with a peeler or mandoline)

Check the manufacturer's manual of your dehydrator for timings.

If you don't have a dehydrator, simply preheat the oven to its lowest setting, around 90–100°C (225°F/gas mark ¼). Spread your slices or ribbons on a lined baking sheet so they are not touching each other and bake for up to 8–12 hours, or until dry and crispy.

Notes
- Don't cut your fruit and vegetables too thin as they may shrivel up and brown; cut too thick they will take forever to dehydrate. I recommend 1-2mm (¹⁄₃₂-¹⁄₁₆in) thick.
- Leave the peels on citrus, apples and pears so they hold their shape better.
- Try blitzing very dry dehydrated fruits and vegetables into a fine dust in your food processor. Use as decoration, sprinkled onto cakes, like a pretty bright strawberry dust circled around the top outer rim of a cake. Or dehydrate beetroot (beets) and horseradish, blend and dust onto popcorn as a natural flavouring. Or try celery blended and mixed with salt for a topping for eggs.

Housekeeping

To sterilize jars and lids

First, wash them in hot soapy water, then rinse in hot water and drip-dry upside down. Next, place them right-side up in a 100°C (225°F/gas mark ¼) oven for at least 20 minutes. Do this before you start cooking. Bacteria dies at temperatures of over 100°C/212°F, so if the jars are filled with hot jam and chutney while everything is at or slightly over this temperature, when you seal the jars nothing should survive.

For fermentation and pickling, cool your sterilized jars before filling. The salts and vinegars in the recipe should provide the correct adverse environment for unwanted bacteria.

You can put your jars and lids into a dishwasher; however, they will still need to be rinsed with hot water afterwards as dishwasher rinse aid can leave a residue that can act as a possible contaminant.

Eggs

All recipes were tested with UK medium and large eggs. Sizes vary in different countries, so bear this in mind.

If you find yourself with an excess of egg whites, these can be frozen. Freeze separately in an ice-cube tray, so you know they're single portions. Defrost in the fridge before use.

Fresh produce

Wash all fruit and vegetables before prepping and chopping as general good practice.

Citrus

Where citrus zests, rinds, peels and skins are used, it's best to go for unwaxed varieties. This way, you are not consuming the heavy wax sprays they put on the fruit to aid longevity. Always use unwaxed fruit where a recipe asks for zest or if the rind is in the food (like marmalade).

Clingflim (plastic wrap)

Where clingflim might be used in a lot of recipe books to keep things fresh, or so things don't develop a skin, I hope that you can make the change to beeswax fabric food wraps, baking paper or lidded airtight Tupperware as alternatives. **beegreenwraps.co.uk**

Composting

If you don't have composting available in your area, then I highly recommend a home wormery. You don't have to have an outdoor area as they don't omit much odour and you can get indoor composters that use grains rather than worms. Think of the amazing by-product of soil and fertilizer for your house plants.

pH testers/meters

These can be used to test the acidity levels in your preserves if you are worried about whether they are safe for consumption. These are widely and cheaply available online. Choose a drink- or food-grade one.

Cupboard staples

Spices/nuts/seeds/kernels/florals/dried fruits

I love to have a variety of flavour additions, or nuts and seeds to play with.
I often buy mine online at:
justingredients.co.uk
buywholefoodsonline.co.uk

Specialist herbs/floral/essences/extracts

For the harder-to-find ingredients, such as dried hibiscus, cacao nibs, rose
extract, try sites that are more chef-aimed:
souschef.co.uk

Gochugaru (Korean red pepper powder)

Used for making kimchi. Try your local Korean food stores or:
thespicery.com
souschef.co.uk

Adobo chillies/paste/chipotle

For Mexican-style hot chillies and pastes, go to Mexican food stores or try:
mexgrocer.co.uk
souschef.co.uk
thespicery.com

Rapid-set pectin

If you are finding it hard to set certain fruits into jams, try:
meridianstar.co.uk

Alternative flours

For strong (bread), spelt, wholemeal, rye, buckwheat or wheat-free flours, try:
shipton-mill.com
dovesfarm.co.uk

For fine polenta or maize (fine corn) flour, which is different from the
cornflour (cornstarch) used for thickening sauces or gravy, try Mexican
shops. I like to use the Maseca brand, where you can get blue and white
varieties, for tortillas. Or Shipton Mill do a good organic maize flour which is
great for cornbread:
mexgrocer.co.uk
shipton-mill.com

Vinegar

I've always been a fan of Aspall vinegars. They still use a traditional method of fermenting their vinegar, it's widely available in most stores, and they create a good base (especially if you are using a lot for pickling and chutney and don't want to use any specialized vinegars):
aspall.co.uk

Fruit/vegetables

Try to buy regionally grown fruit and veg that has been farmed with a low carbon footprint. Follow the seasons and eat seasonally. Buy from local markets, organic where you can, or sprayed with minimal pesticides. Make a conscious decision about where and who you are supporting by voting with your money.

Meat/fish/poultry/dairy

Once again, try to buy regionally/locally. Always buy free-range. Become friends with your local butcher/fishmonger, so you know where your meat/fish/poultry/eggs are being reared (or caught). Ask your fishmonger what seafood they sell that is certified sustainable. Dairy is a massive industry, so find smaller farmed milks/butters/cheeses or use plant-based alternatives and ones that are better for the environment (such as oat-based products rather than almond-based ones). Buy hand- and locally made from your local market. We can make change through supply and demand by consciously buying within these industries.

Wood chips

For oak and hickory chips for smoking, try:
nisbets.co.uk
hotsmoked.co.uk

Index

Index *continued*

Thank you

Firstly, thank you for buying this book. It's a small step into the world of thinking about food sustainability and how to make the most of natural resources.

Making a recipe book is a collaboration – it is moulded and made beautiful along the way – so I must thank those who have made this a better book than I could ever have done by myself. Céline Hughes and Claire Rochford and the team at Quadrille, sorry for the madness; thank you for the calmness and sanity. Laura Edwards, your gentle appreciation of *chiaroscuro*, just wow. Rosie Ramsden and Anna Wilkins, for creating the bigger, better picture. Assistants Kitty Coles and Lucinda Hankin, massive thanks.

Special thanks to Louise Stapley and Mina Holland for looking over my words before sending them to my editor, making sure I was on my way in the right direction. You both have skills that I admire and am quite frankly envious of.

For continuous support and recipe testing from friends: Felicity Spector (you are a constant and always), Uyen Luu (for our good rants), Henrietta Inman (for pastry genius), Sanaz Zardosht (love you crazy one), Safia Shakarchi (your precision and eye for detail), Louise Stapley (again), my family (Mum, Kate [mum-in-law] and my sister Jakki), and thanks to those of you who reached out via Instagram and helped along the way.

Big thanks to my staff who have supported me and the dream of Newton & Pott on its rollercoaster journey to the end of its ride. I know working with a crazy, passionate Kiwi can't be easy at the best of times.

Mum, Auntie Cher, Naomi Devlin, Edd Kimber, Diana Neto, Karolina Stein, Chris Leach, Michael (Tee) Thompson, Taj Cambridge and Oliver Rowe for your friendship, love, support and recipe advice. Without you guys, my knowledge and understanding of how things work, in life and food, would be lost.

Thank you to Heather Holden-Brown and Elly James at HHB Agency – without your guidance this book would have never come to fruition. And to all the people who have helped me along the way with my food career, from collaborations to publications, too many to list.

Lastly, to my husband (designer of this book and my last: *The Modern Preserver*). Mark, thank you for always, always, making me feel like a queen, invincible and unstoppable. Your love and support make me a stronger person. Without you, none of this would ever have been realized. I adore you, admire you, you are my world.

About the author

Kylee Newton grew up in New Zealand and lives in London. She has turned her hand to a variety of creative jobs from analogue photography printing for artist Wolfgang Tillmans to floristry in jam jars. Many years ago, she began making preserves to give as homemade Christmas presents, which led her to create the London-based preserving company Newton & Pott. Making quality jams, pickles and chutneys in small batches was at its heart, selling them at local London markets and with clients such as Selfridges, Harrods and Harvey Nichols. She is an expert in her field and now focuses her attention on hosting preserving workshops, food writing, food consultation and recipe development. *The Modern Preserver's Kitchen* is her second book.

Publishing Director: Sarah Lavelle
Senior Commissioning Editor: Céline Hughes
Design: High-low.studio
Senior Designer: Katherine Keeble
Photographer: Laura Edwards
Food Stylist: Rosie Ramsden
Food Stylist Assistants: Kitty Coles and
Lucinda Hankin
Prop Stylist: Anna Wilkins
Head of Production: Stephen Lang
Senior Production Controller: Nikolaus Ginelli

Published in 2021 by Quadrille,
an imprint of Hardie Grant Publishing

Quadrille
52–54 Southwark Street
London SE1 1UN
quadrille.com

Cataloguing in Publication Data: a catalogue
record for this book is available from the
British Library.

ISBN 978 1 78713 538 3

Printed in China